2003

Clara,
   Congratulations
on the baut Mitzvah
      Nicholas

The Jews in Early America

A Chronicle of Good Taste and Good Deeds

Sandra Cumings Malamed

FITHIAN PRESS, MCKINLEYVILLE, CALIFORNIA · 2003

Book design and typography: Studio E Books,
Santa Barbara, CA   www.studio-e-books.com

Published by Fithian Press
A division of Daniel and Daniel, Publishers, Inc.
Post Office Box 2790
McKinleyville, CA 95519
www.danielpublishing.com

LIBRARY OF CONGRESS CATALOGING-IN-PUBLICATION DATA
Malamed, Sandra Cumings, (date)
  The Jews in early America : a chronicle of good taste and good deeds / by Sandra Cumings
Malamed.
     p. cm.
  ISBN 1-56474-408-6 (cloth : alk. paper) — ISBN 1-56474-407-8 (pbk. : alk. paper)
  1. Jews—United States—History—17th century. 2. Jews—United States—History—18th
century. 3. Jews—United States—History—19th century. 4. Jews—United States—Biogra-
phy. I. Title.
E184.3512.M35 2003
973'.04924—dc21
                  2002151262

In honor of my family

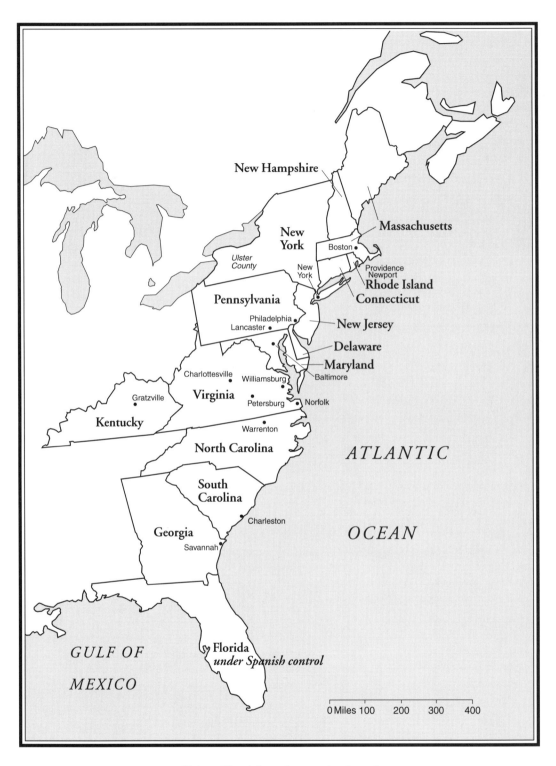

Cities of Jewish settlement in America

Contents

Preface and Acknowledgments 9

Introduction 17
    How Jewish Life in America Began

Luis Moses Gomez 27
    The Oldest Jewish House in America

Abigail Franks 31
    She Challenged Her Jewish Community to Reform

Myer Myers 39
    A Thing of Beauty Is a Joy Forever

The Touro Synagogue of Newport 51
    The Oldest Standing Synagogue in America

The Rivera–Lopez Family of Newport 57
    From Marranos to Prominent Merchants

Dr. John de Sequeyra 65
    A Pioneer in the Treatment of the Insane

The Gratz Family 75
    Early Pioneers of Westward Expansion

Joseph Simon 83
    Entrepreneur, Frontiersman, and Patriot

Abigail Minis 87
    An Early American Innkeeper

The Sheftalls of Savannah 95
    Heroes of the Revolution

Haym Salomon 101
    He Helped Finance the American Revolution

Moses Michael Hays 107
    A Boston Businessman

The Cohens and the Ettings 113
    They Brought Jewish Society to Baltimore

Gershom Mendes Seixas 119
    Spiritual Leader for Shearith Israel

The Moses Myers Family 123
    A Family Home in Norfolk, for Many Generations

The Richmond Jewish Community 135
    The Importance of Religious Freedom

Four Early American Women 147
    History Revealed Through Women's Words

Mordecai Manuel Noah 153
    Diplomat, Writer, and Political Philosopher

Uriah Phillips Levy 159
    He Saved Monticello

Isaac Leeser 167
    The First Jewish-American Publisher

Solomon Nunes Carvalho 173
    Photographer of the Frontier

Conclusion 181
    Good Taste and Good Deeds

Bibliography 189

Index 191

Preface and Acknowledgments

IN 1607, the first permanent European settlement in America was founded at Jamestown, Virginia. The story of the people who were part of that experience has been written about and retold over and over throughout our nation's history.

In 1620, the Pilgrims came from England to Plymouth, Massachusetts and established another community. Their story has also been preserved and retold and celebrated over and over.

In 1654, another settlement of European immigrants was established in New Amsterdam, which has since become New York. These people were Jewish, and theirs was the first Jewish-American community. Their story is far less known than the stories of Jamestown and Plymouth, and the same can be said about the early Jewish-American communities of Philadelphia, Savannah, Baltimore, Newport, Charleston, and elsewhere. Jews made a vital contribution to the establishment, growth, and prosperity of many early American communities. To a large extent those contributions have been overlooked by American historians, and that is the reason for this book.

In 1989, the Skirball Museum in Los Angeles asked me to deliver a series of lectures on the American Jewish Colonial experience. I became fascinated with the research involved and totally immersed myself in the project, which taught me so much about both American history and Jewish culture. I developed more than twenty lectures, which I have presented to hundreds of audiences throughout the United States. It is now with both pleasure and pride—pride in my remarkable Jewish forbears—that I present this information, which was taken from those lectures, accompanied by photographs that beautifully illustrate the life styles of these early Jewish Americans.

I wish to gratefully acknowledge all the many institutions that have helped me in the research and writing of this book. They include the following historical societies: The American Jewish Historical Society, Waltham, Massachusetts; The New York Historical Society, New York, New York; The Georgia Historical Society, Savannah, Georgia; The Newport Historical Society, Newport,

Rhode Island; The Maryland Historical Society, Baltimore, Maryland; The Historical Society of Pennsylvania, Philadelphia, Pennsylvania; The South Carolina Historical Society, Charleston, South Carolina; The Virginia Historical Society, Richmond, Virginia; and The Jewish Historical Society of Maryland, Baltimore, Maryland.

For synagogue and cemetery records, I am grateful to the following Jewish congregations: Congregation Shearith Israel, New York, New York; Touro Synagogue, Newport, Rhode Island; the Congregation Mikveh Israel Synagogue, Philadelphia, Pennsylvania; Beth Elohim Synagogue, Charleston, South Carolina; Mickve Israel Synagogue, Savannah, Georgia; and Congregation Beth Ahaba, Richmond, Virginia.

I wish to thank the following museums: The Philadelphia Art Museum, in Philadelphia, Pennsylvania; The Metropolitan Art Museum in New York, New York; The Valentine Museum, Richmond, Virginia; Telfair Academy of Arts and Sciences, Savannah, Georgia; Colonial Williamsburg, Williamsburg, Virginia; The Moses Myers House, Norfolk, Virginia; The National Jewish Museum, Philadelphia, Pennsylvania; The Corning Museum, Corning, New York; Winterthur House Museum, Wilmington, Delaware; Elfreth's Alley Association, Philadelphia, Pennsylvania; The Fairmont Park Historical Preservation Trust, Philadelphia, Pennsylvania; The Germantown Historical Society, Philadelphia, Pennsylvania; The Museum of the City of New York, New York, New York; Monticello Museum and Gardens, Charlottesville, Virginia; and the D.A.R. Museum of Washington, D.C.

I am especially grateful to the following archives and libraries: The Swem Library of the College of William and Mary, Williamsburg, Virginia; The United States Archives, Washington, D.C.; The American Jewish Archives, Cincinnati, Ohio; The Naval Archives, Washington, D.C.; Hebrew Union College Library, University of Southern California, Los Angeles, California and Cincinnati, Ohio; The Naval Archives of Pennsylvania, Philadelphia, Pennsylvania; The Pennsylvania Academy of the Arts, Philadelphia, Pennsylvania; The Redwood Library Association, Newport, Rhode Island; Brown University Library, Providence, Rhode Island; Harvard University Archives, Cambridge, Massachusetts; The Archives of the Portuguese Israelite Synagogue, Amsterdam, Holland; The Archives of Bevis Marks Synagogue, London, England; The Archives of Columbia University, New York, New York; and The University of Georgia Library, Athens, Georgia.

I am of course deeply grateful to all the many, many people who assisted and encouraged me throughout this project. They include: Bernard Wax, Director Emeritus, Michael Feldberg, Director, and Stanley Remsberg, Assistant

Director of the American Jewish Historical Society; Morrison Hecksher, Curator of the Metropolitan Museum of Art; Bernard Kusinitz, Archivist in Memoriam of Touro Synagogue; Soloman Breibart, Archivist of Beth Elohim Synagogue; Janice Ovadiah, Director of Shearith Israel Congregation; Heather Ventors, Jennifer Goldborough, and Jeff Goldblum of the Maryland Historical Society; Margaret Cook of the Swem Library at the College of William and Mary; Kevin Profitt of The American Jewish Archives in Cincinnati, Ohio; Barbara Batson, Assistant Director of the Valentine Museum, Richmond, Virginia; J. Patrick Brennan, Director of the Moses Myers House in Norfolk, Virginia; Jane Spillman and Arlene Palmer Schwind of the Corning Museum in Corning, New York; Dr. Leo Herskovitz of New York, New York; Mrs. Marion Levy Abrams of Savannah, Georgia; Mrs. Ruth H. Schulson of New York, New York; Mrs. Grace Grossman, Curator of the Skirball Museum in Los Angeles; Elissa Kayne of the Philadelphia Academy of Fine Arts; Mrs. Davida Deutsch of New York, New York; Martha W. Rowe of the Museum of Early Southern Decorative Arts in Winston-Salem, North Carolina; Jeff Flannery of the Library of Congress, Manuscript Division; Sally and Peter Rabinowitz Solis-Cohen of Philadelphia; Lauren E. Simeone of Philadelphia; Martha L. Mitchell, Librarian of the Brown University Library; Susan Stein of the Monticello Museum and Gardens; Lyn Kelsey and Joan Selby of Congregation Beth Ahaba, Richmond, Virginia; Hollee Haswell, Curator of Columbia University; Bettie L. Kerr, Officer of Lexington Kentucky Fayette Urban County Government; Jack Lindsay, Curator of the Fine Arts Museum of Philadelphia; Nonna Rubin, Curator of Elfreth's Alley Association in Philadelphia; Bert Denker of the Winterthur Museum and Gardens in Wilmington, Delaware; Christine Minter-Dowd, Director of the D.A.R. Museum in Washington, D.C.; Rabbi Saul J. Rubin of Savannah, Georgia; Thomas E. Camden, Head Librarian of the University of Georgia; Virginia Du Vall, Curator of the Jewish Historical Society of Maryland; Elliot Meadows of the New York Historical Society; Danielle M. Green, Curator of the Harvard University Archives; and Harold B. Gill, Historian, Colonial Williamsburg Foundation.

Most of all, I want to thank my dear friends Karen, Amanda, and Brandon Matloff, and Mrs. Regina Holt, Mary Jo Chevalier, Deborah Green, and of course my wonderful family, whose help and encouragement made this whole book possible. Thanks to my two children, I now have a valuable collection of thousands of slides of Jewish colonial artifacts. My daughter, Elizabeth Malamed, has traveled extensively with me throughout the former colonies and Europe, with her keen artistic eye, capturing on film whatever treasures we found. My son, Laird Malamed, took all of the pictures sent to me by museums and historical societies and made them into slides as well. Laird also put my lectures onto a database for use in my computer and created my marketing materials. I am forever grateful to my beloved daughter-in-law, Rebecca Malamed, and to my grandson, Justin Malamed, and my dear friend Eric Biederman for their support, interest, and encouragement. And of course my greatest thanks to my sponsor and biggest fan during all of this vast undertaking, my husband, Kenneth Malamed.

There are no words to thank all of these people sufficiently for their loving support. I have always said that I began this project in order to better understand my own rich Jewish heritage, which I love and respect. That love and respect for my Judaic background I owe to my grandparents, Lena Cumings and Bertha and Charles Caper; to my parents, Charles Cumings and Shirley Caper Cumings; to my mother-in-law and father-in-law, Reba and Daniel Malamed; and to two adopted parents whose encouragement was always there, Elaine and Bill Greenberg.

ILLUSTRATION CREDITS

Frontispiece, map of the colonies prepared by Mary Jo Chevalier;

Page 17, statue of Moses Maimonides, courtesy of the Spanish Embassy and the Historical Society of Cordoba, Spain;

P. 18, tortures of the Inquisition, courtesy of the Department of Special Collections, the University of Notre Dame;

P. 19, Amsterdam synagogue, from *Book on Religious Celebrations,* by B. Picart, from the collection of Sandra and Kenneth Malamed, photograph by Laird Malamed;

P. 19, marketplace in Recife, by Jose Antonio Goncalves de Mello, courtesy of Arquivo Historico, Judaico de Pernambuco, Recife, Pernambuco, Brazil;

P. 22, wedding glass etched by Lazarus Isaacs, courtesy of Corning Glass Museum, Corning, NY;

P. 24, synagogue in Recife, interior, photo by Fritz Simons;

P. 24, portrait of Moses Levy, courtesy of the American Jewish Historical Society, Waltham, MA, and New York, NY;

P. 27, portrait of Isaac Gomez, courtesy of the American Jewish Historical Society, Waltham, MA, and New York, NY;

P. 29, Gomez Mill House, courtesy of the American Jewish Historical Society, Waltham, MA, and New York, NY;

P. 31, portrait of Abigail Franks, courtesy of the American Jewish Historical Society, Waltham, MA, and New York, NY;

P. 32, Shearith Israel, Mill Street, courtesy of the American Jewish Historical Society, Waltham, MA, and New York, NY;

P. 33, portrait of Jacob Franks, courtesy of the American Jewish Historical Society, Waltham, MA, and New York, NY;

P. 37, portrait of David and Richa Franks, courtesy of the American Jewish Historical Society, Waltham, MA, and New York, NY;

P. 39, Myer Myers sugar bowl, from the collection of Sandra and Kenneth Malamed, photograph by Laird Malamed;

P. 42, Rimmonim by Myer Myers, courtesy of the American Jewish Historical Society, Waltham, MA, and New York, NY;

P. 43, Myer Myers tablespoon, front and back, from the collection of Sandra and Kenneth Malamed, photograph by Laird Malamed;

P. 48, Myer Myers tankard, from the collection of Sandra and Kenneth Malamed, photograph by Laird Malamed;

P. 49, Philadelphia synagogue daybook page, courtesy of the American Jewish Historical Society, Waltham, MA, and New York, NY;

P. 51, Touro Synagogue, interior, courtesy of the American Jewish Historical Society, Waltham, MA, and New York, NY;

P. 52, Touro Synagogue, exterior, courtesy of the American Jewish Historical Society, Waltham, MA, and New York, NY;

P. 54, portrait of Judah Touro, courtesy of the American Jewish Historical Society, Waltham, MA, and New York, NY;

P. 55, Touro Synagogue cemetery, courtesy of the American Jewish Historical Society, Waltham, MA, and New York, NY;

P. 57, portrait of Jacob Rodriguez Rivera, courtesy of the American Jewish Historical Society, Waltham, MA, and New York, NY;

P. 59, circumcision set, courtesy of the American Jewish Historical Society, Waltham, MA, and New York, NY;

P. 60, portrait of Aaron Lopez, courtesy of the American Jewish Historical Society, Waltham, MA, and New York, NY;

P. 62, bill of sale to Aaron Lopez, courtesy of the American Jewish Historical Society, Waltham, MA, and New York, NY;

P. 65, portrait of John de Sequeyra, courtesy of Colonial Williamsburg Foundation, Abby Aldrich Rockefeller Folk Art Museum, Williamsburg, VA;

P. 68, medical instruments, courtesy of Colonial Williamsburg Foundation, Abby Aldrich Rockefeller Folk Art Museum, Williamsburg, VA;

P. 70, public hospital in Williamsburg, courtesy of Colonial Williamsburg Foundation, Abby Aldrich Rockefeller Folk Art Museum, Williamsburg, VA;

P. 71, patient room, courtesy of Colonial Williamsburg Foundation, Abby Aldrich Rockefeller Folk Art Museum, Williamsburg, VA;

P. 75, portrait of Michael Gratz, courtesy of the American Jewish Historical Society, Waltham, MA, and New York, NY;

P. 76, Liberty Bell, courtesy of the American Jewish Historical Society, Waltham, MA, and New York, NY;

P. 78, Gratz hekscher, courtesy of the American Jewish Historical Society, Waltham, MA, and New York, NY;

P. 80, chest and chair owned by Michael Gratz, courtesy of Winterthur Museum, Winterthur, DE;

P. 81, portrait of Rebecca Gratz. courtesy of the American Jewish Historical Society, Waltham, MA, and New York, NY;

P. 84, Joseph Simon's Ark lintel, courtesy of the American Jewish Historical Society, Waltham, MA, and New York, NY;

P. 85, Joseph Simon's will, courtesy of Lancaster County Historical Society, Lancaster, PA;

P. 87, Philip Minis's silver chalice, courtesy of Georgia Historical Society, Savannah, GA;

P. 91, Philip Minis's spurs, courtesy of Georgia Historical Society, Savannah, GA;

P. 92, portrait of Judith Polock Minis, courtesy of Mickve Israel, Savannah, GA ;

P. 95, portrait of Mordecai Sheftall, courtesy of Marion Levy Abrams, Savannah, GA;

P. 96, portrait of Frances Sheftall, courtesy of Marion Levy Abrams, Savannah, GA;

P. 97, Old Jewish Burial Ground, photo by Ed Jackson, Savannah, GA;

P. 98, portrait of Nellie Bush Sheftall, courtesy of the American Jewish Historical Society, Waltham, MA, and New York, NY;

P. 101, portrait of Haym Salomon, courtesy of the American Jewish Historical Society, Waltham, MA, and New York, NY;

P. 102, Synagogue Mikveh Israel, courtesy of the American Jewish Historical Society, Waltham, MA, and New York, NY;

P. 103, portrait of Samuel Hays, from the collection of Sandra and Kenneth Malamed, photograph by Laird Malamed;

P. 104, statue of Morris, Washington, and Salomon, courtesy of the American Jewish Historical Society, Waltham, MA, and New York, NY;

P. 106, letter from Haym Salomon to James Madison, from the collection of Sandra and Kenneth Malamed, photograph by Laird Malamed;

P. 107, portrait of Moses Michael Hays, courtesy of the American Jewish Historical Society, Waltham, MA, and New York, NY;

P. 109, letter from Moses Michael Hays, from the collection of Sandra and Kenneth Malamed, photograph by Laird Malamed;

P. 111, silver teapot made by Paul Revere, courtesy of Museum of Fine Arts, Boston, MA;

P. 113, miniature of Rachel Gratz Etting, courtesy of the American Jewish Historical Society, Waltham, MA, and New York, NY;

P. 114, childhood portrait of J. Marx Etting, from the collection of Sandra and Kenneth Malamed, photograph by Laird Malamed;

P. 115, silhouette of Salomon Etting, courtesy of the American Jewish Historical Society, Waltham, MA, and New York, NY;

P. 117, "The Jew Bill," courtesy of the American Jewish Historical Society, Waltham, MA, and New York, NY;

P. 119, portrait of Gershom Mendes Seixas, courtesy of the American Jewish Historical Society, Waltham, MA, and New York, NY;

P. 121, Chatham Square Cemetery, courtesy of the American Jewish Historical Society, Waltham, MA, and New York, NY;

P. 122, Gershom Mendes Seixas's gravestone, courtesy of the American Jewish Historical Society, Waltham, MA, and New York, NY;

P. 123, Gilbert Stuart portrait of Moses Myers, courtesy of the Chrysler Museum, Norfolk, VA;

P. 124, portrait of Eliza Myers, courtesy of the Chrysler Museum, Norfolk, VA;

P. 127, Moses Myers House, exterior, courtesy of the Chrysler Museum, Norfolk, VA;

P. 129, Moses Myers House dining room, courtesy of the Chrysler Museum, Norfolk, VA;

P. 130, Moses Myers House music room, courtesy of the Chrysler Museum, Norfolk, VA;

P. 135, portrait of Jacob I. Cohen, courtesy of Maryland Historical Society, Baltimore;

P. 137, Religious Freedom Act, from the book *Notes on the State of Virginia* by Thomas Jefferson, from the collection of Laird M. Malamed, photographed by Laird M. Malamed;

P. 139, map of Virginia, from the book *Notes on the State of Virginia* by Thomas Jefferson, from the collection of Laird M. Malamed, photographed by Laird M. Malamed;

P. 143, Beth Shalom Synagogue, courtesy of the American Jewish Historical Society, Waltham, MA, and New York, NY;

P. 144, portrait of Judith Hays Myers, courtesy of Richmond History Center, VA;

P. 145, portrait of Samuel Myers, courtesy of Richmond History Center, VA;

P. 147, portrait of Grace Seixas Nathan, courtesy of the American Jewish Historical Society, Waltham, MA, and New York, NY;

P. 149, portrait of Miriam Gratz, courtesy of the American Jewish Historical Society, Waltham, MA, and New York, NY;

P. 150, portrait of Frances Isaacs Hendricks, courtesy of Museum of the City of New York, bequest of Alma H. Harwood;

P. 153, portrait of Mordecai Manuel Noah, from the book *Travels in England, France and Spain* by Mordecai Manuel Noah, from the collection of Sandra and Kenneth Malamed, photograph by Laird Malamed;

P. 154, *Travels in England, France, Spain…,* from the collection of Sandra and Kenneth Malamed, photograph by Laird Malamed;

P. 156, drawing of Mordecai Manuel Noah, courtesy of the American Jewish Historical Society, Waltham, MA, and New York, NY;

P. 157, *Discourse on the Evidences of the American Indian…,* from *Travels in the West* by Solomon Carvalho, from the collection of Sandra and Kenneth Malamed, photograph by Laird Malamed;

P. 159, portrait of Uriah Phillips Levy, courtesy of the American Jewish Historical Society, Waltham, MA, and New York, NY;

P. 163, Monticello, courtesy of Monticello/Thomas Jefferson Foundation, Inc.;

P. 164, gravestone of Rachel Phillips Levy, courtesy of Monticello/Thomas Jefferson Foundation, Inc.;

P. 165, portrait of Commodore Levy, courtesy of the American Jewish Historical Society, Waltham, MA, and New York, NY;

P. 166, Uriah P. Levy Chapel, courtesy of the American Jewish Historical Society, Waltham, MA, and New York, NY;

P. 167, portrait of Isaac Leeser, courtesy of the American Jewish Historical Society, Waltham, MA, and New York, NY;

P. 168, Mikveh Israel Synagogue, interior, drawing by Lauren E. Simeone ;

P. 169, Mikveh Israel Synagogue, exterior, drawing by Lauren E. Simeone ;

P. 170, *Instructions in the Mosaic Religion,* from the collection of Sandra and Kenneth Malamed, photograph by Laird Malamed;

P. 171, *The Occident,* from the collection of Sandra and Kenneth Malamed, photograph by Laird Malamed;

P. 173, portrait of Solomon Nunes Carvalho, courtesy of the American Jewish Historical Society, Waltham, MA, and New York, NY;

P. 174, Beth Elohim Synagogue, interior, courtesy of the American Jewish Historical Society, Waltham, MA, and New York, NY;

P. 175, Beth Elohim Synagogue, exterior, courtesy of the American Jewish Historical Society, Waltham, MA, and New York, NY;

P. 177, pages from Carvalho book, from the collection of Sandra and Kenneth Malamed, photograph by Laird Malamed;

P. 181, indigo production, courtesy of the South Carolina Historical Society, Charleston, SC;

P. 182, poem by Penïna Moïse, photographed by Mary Jo Chevalier;

P. 183, handbill for *The Merchant of Venice,* courtesy of Colonial Williamsburg Foundation, Abby Aldrich Rockefeller Folk Art Museum, Williamsburg, VA;

P. 184, plaque commemorating Francis Salvador, courtesy of the South Carolina Historical Society, Charleston, SC;

pp. 186-187, copy of George Washington letter, from the collection of Sandra and Kenneth Malamed, photograph by Laird Malamed.

The Jews in Early America

Introduction

*How Jewish Life in
America Began*

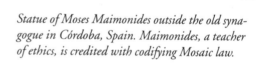

THE history of the American colonial Jew does not begin in America. In a sense, it is not a beginning at all, but the climax to a struggle that began with roots in the Iberian Peninsula some 1400 years ago in Córdoba, Spain.

There, Jews lived relatively peacefully with their Muslim neighbors. It was an age of the flowering of Jewish culture in art,

Statue of Moses Maimonides outside the old syna-gogue in Córdoba, Spain. Maimonides, a teacher of ethics, is credited with codifying Mosaic law.

architecture, poetry, and philosophy. There were great academies where the Talmud was studied. Maimonides, the rabbi responsible for the codification of all Jewish Mosaic law, lived during this period.

Change came in the fourteenth century, when Christianity moved in. The Christians took over the power in Spain and, city by city, persecuted the Jewish population. The order was given: every Jew must convert to Christianity or die. In order to escape death and yet still be true to their own code, many Jews publicly converted to the Christian faith, but secretly practiced their Judaism at home. These people became known as the "secret ones," or "Marranos," the Spanish word for pigs.

In 1478, a court system was formed in Spain to rid the country of these Marranos. This court was referred to as the "Inquisition." Its methods were cruel; torture and death were its tools. When these methods were still not enough to change the minds of the Marranos about becoming complete Christians, the court insisted that the Jews be banished from Spain altogether. In 1492, Queen Isabella and King Ferdinand of Spain complied with the Inquisition's orders, and one hundred fifty thousand Jews were forced to leave Spain forever.

An example of the kinds of torture used on Jewish people and people suspected of celebrating Jewish rights during the Inquisition in both Spain and Portugal. In addition to torture, death was also the punishment of some Jews.

Homeless, these Jews went to Turkey, Greece, Italy, France, and other lands, where they began to rebuild their lives. Many Jews who left Spain at that time went to Portugal, and when the Inquisition caught up with them there, they left for Holland. It is this line of Jews who eventually began the first Jewish communities in America, so it is their history that we will explore now.

Life in Holland was good for the Jew. By 1650, they were afforded many freedoms. They could own land, become employers, practice medicine, and even hold public office. In Amsterdam, Jews were able to build a large, imposing house of worship, the Portuguese Synagogue, which became the center of their life in Holland. Beautiful in its architecture, it was patterned in part after the Second Temple in Israel. Its design would also influence the building and design of the Bevis Marks Portuguese Shul in London and America's own five Portuguese-Spanish synagogues that were established in the early colonial period.

Along with the development of the mercantile trade came Holland's efforts at colonization. This was done through the establishment of the Dutch West India Company—a large portion of which was owned by the successful Jewish community. One of the areas of the world they colonized was Recife, Brazil, which the Dutch had taken away from another maritime power, Portugal. Hundreds of Jewish settlers from Holland came to help colonize Recife and to establish it under Dutch rule. All went as planned until 1654, when the Portuguese reclaimed Recife and immediately ordered the Jews to leave the country in three months' time or convert to Christianity. Again the Jews were being threatened as they had been in Spain and Portugal with an inquisition, and again they were forced to leave their homes. Most of them went back to Amsterdam.

One of the ships bound for Holland was pirated and the people aboard

Above: The interior of the Portuguese Israelite Synagogue, which Jews had the freedom to build in Amsterdam. Shown is a celebration of Simchat Torah, or the rejoicing of the Laws of Moses. This was the parent synagogue of the first six Sephardic synagogues in America.

Below: The marketplace in the Dutch Jewish community of Recife, Pernambuco, Brazil. Here Jews raised sugar cane until 1654, when the land was taken away by Portugal. The Portuguese brought the Inquisition with them, and Jews were forced to choose between conversion to Christianity, death, and flight. The latter was the choice of the twenty-three men, women, and children who started the first "Jewish community" in New Amsterdam in 1654.

were left to die on the open seas. It is miraculous that the French ship, the *Sainte Catherine,* which they were on, still carried the penniless emigrants to another Dutch colony, New Amsterdam, later known under English rule as New York. There were twenty-three Jews in all on that ship. These twenty-three men, women, and children formed the nucleus of the first Jewish community in America.

One would think that these twenty-three Dutch people would have been welcomed into this Dutch community. But they weren't. The governor of this colony, Peter Stuyvesant, wanted no part of having a Jewish community there. He petitioned his employers, the Dutch West India Company in Amsterdam, to have the Jews removed as quickly as possible, because they were "different in their religious preference and attitude." He requested "that the deceitful race, such hateful enemies and blasphemers of the name of Christ, be not allowed further to infect and trouble this new colony, to the detraction of your worships and the dissatisfaction of your worships' most affectionate subjects."

When the petition arrived in Holland, the Dutch were in no mood to grant Stuyvesant's request. They were having problems getting people to colonize the new lands, and here was an eager ready-made group of people who needed no extra incentives to stay and to make New Amsterdam their home. The Dutch needed that kind of activity. Even more important, the Amsterdam Jewish Community by that time owned a sizable amount of the Dutch West India company, and there was no way that the Dutch Jews were going to grant Stuyvesant's wish. In fact, the directors of the company said not only that Jews could stay, but that they could trade freely and travel as long as they took care of their own sick and poor and were not a general burden to the whole community.

And so they stayed, and as their ancestors had done in Holland, they began to build a life for themselves in their new home. And although there were actually individual Jews in the colonies much earlier than those in New Amsterdam, such as Joachim Gaunse of the famed Roanoke colony in Virginia in the 1580s, this new settlement was the first time a group of Jews actually intended to establish a community in America.

Asser Levy was one of the original twenty-three settlers in New Amsterdam in 1654. Having arrived penniless, by the time of his death in February, 1682 he had become a very wealthy merchant. Asser Levy was licensed by the colony of New Amsterdam as a butcher and slaughterer, and he was excused from slaughtering hogs because he was a Jew.

*   *   *

Jews continued to immigrate to America after the first twenty-three people in New Amsterdam. Jews representing both the Spanish-Portuguese (Sephardim) and the German or European (Ashkenazim) came during the colonial period and in the Federal era, from 1654 to 1815. In addition to New Amsterdam (New York), these Jewish families colonized four other cities—Newport, Rhode Island in 1660 and 1750; Charleston, South Carolina in 1695; Savannah, Georgia in 1733; and Philadelphia, Pennsylvania in 1737. All of these four other cities were much more hospitable to the Jews than New Amsterdam had been.

It is important to note that these five cities, all on major waterways, were centers of commerce and industry. Most of the Jewish population in the colonies—about ninety percent—were in the mercantile trade, which required water access for shipping. The remaining ten percent of colonial Jews were involved in various other vocations, including farming, medicine, and the arts.

In addition to these five main cities, there were also other places where Jews lived during colonial times. These places often had only one family or a small group of Jewish people, not really enough to be called a large community. They included Lancaster and York, Pennsylvania; Baltimore, Maryland; Warrenton, North Carolina; Richmond, Charlottesville, Norfolk, and Williamsburg, Virginia; and Boston, Massachusetts.

Even though America's Jewish population grew, the numbers remained comparatively small. By 1776, there were about 2,500 Jews in America, which amounted to less than one-tenth of a percent of the total population. By 1790, when the first national census was taken, the Jewish population was distributed like this:

Newport, Rhode Island, 76; New England, 150
New York, New York, 246; New York State, 350
Philadelphia, Pennsylvania, 122; Pennsylvania, 250
Charleston, South Carolina, 188; South Carolina, 300
Richmond, Virginia, 28; Virginia, 200
Savannah, Georgia, 15; Georgia, 100

Jewish immigration in this early time of American history was limited. Except for the development of the communities of Newport, where fifteen Dutch, Spanish, and Portuguese families came in 1660, and Savannah, where ninety people arrived in 1733, most Jews came one or two families at a time, or even as single individuals.

* * *

There was a broad spectrum of experience possible for the Jews in the colonial and the early national eras in America. In this new world, Jews were given much greater freedom to participate in society than they had in Europe. This freedom of opportunity can best be seen in the ability of the colonial Jews to earn their livelihoods as merchants, traders, doctors, journalists and artists. Jews were also barbers, braziers, candlemakers, snuffmakers, tailors, tobacconists, peddlers, shopkeepers, and even slave traders.

For example, there was one Lazarus Isaac, a glass cutter who came from England in 1773 and hired out as a flowerer and a cutter for the now famous Stiegel Glassworks of Lancaster, Pennsylvania. On a copy of his contract, his name is signed in Hebrew, Lazar bar Yitzak Sgl (Segal). His work was so well respected, so excellent and meticulous, that when Stiegel's own daughter was to be married, Isaac was given the job and the honor of etching the official wedding glass.

Wedding glass etched by Lazarus Isaacs when he worked for Stiegel Glassworks of Pennsylvania. This glass, made for Stiegel's own daughter, is housed today at the Corning Glass Museum in Corning, New York.

Beyond the economic opportunities, Jewish immigrants discovered that it was possible to become members of their new American society and still retain their Jewish traditions. Here we see Jewish participants in the cultural scene of colonial life, such as Moses Franks, who was a member of the Redwood Library Literary Club in Newport, Rhode Island, and also an active member of his religious affiliation, Touro Synagogue. Another example of cultural participation was Myer Myers, the famous Jewish-American silversmith, who was also the president of his synagogue, Shearith Israel, in New York City. With their religious and cultural activities running side by side, the colonial Jews were able to reach out to the larger scope of their communities with jobs in local governments and nonsectarian organizations. A good example is Mordecai Sheftall of Savannah, Georgia, who served in the legislative body of the State of Georgia and as an active member of the Union Society of Georgia, which his father, Benjamin, had helped to form in 1750 to further the education of orphaned children.

Jews even became leaders in shaping the policies and running the government at the national level. Haym Salomon, for example, helped George Washington raise money to finance the Revolutionary War. The Gratz brothers of Philadelphia, Barnard and Michael, helped organize and signed the Non-Importation Resolution against the tax-levying British monarchy.

In all of these areas—economic, cultural, and political—the new freedom of the colonial Jews gave them the chance to make valuable contributions to the birth and growth of their new home, America. Their challenges were many: to have Sephardim and Ashkenazim from completely different cultural backgrounds and traditions live side by side in understanding and cooperation; to have Jewish rights accepted in a basically Christian society without prejudice; and the most important challenge, to maintain and cultivate their distinctly Jewish traditions without assimilation in a basically open society where Christians and Jews often came together for economic, social, and political reasons.

Naturally the culture of the early American Jewish community was strongly influenced by the European countries from which they had come, Portugal, Spain, Holland, Germany, Poland, and England. We can see European influence in the design of their synagogues and cemeteries and in their ritual practices and their moral and ethical codes. Often when members of the new American colonial Jewish communities did not feel they had enough knowledge to decide a particular issue of religious law at their synagogue, they would turn to what they considered their parent synagogues in Amsterdam and London.

However, Jewish culture was also influenced by the culture of the new land. Portraits of colonial Jews show them to have learned well how to look in America, for they wholeheartedly adopted the dress of the period. These observant Jews learned to speak English and dress like their neighbors, whose designs came directly from the English. Men affected the waistcoats, knee-breeches, powdered hair, buckled shoes, and the ruffled shirts of the period. The women were dressed in the most beautiful silks, satins, and velvets, adorned with lace on the bodice and the sleeves. Their houses and furnishings also looked like those of their neighbors.

Right from the very beginning, Jewish people were concerned not only with their own needs, but also with those of the community around them. For example, Moses Levy was one of the most important merchants in all of the

Above: Reconstructed interior of the Dutch Jewish Synagogue in Recife. When the Portuguese took over Recife in 1654, they destroyed the original synagogue building on this site. The reconstruction is Sephardic in style. Within is the newly discovered mikve *or ritual bath.*

Right: Moses Levy, a wealthy merchant from the New York colony, shown in three-quarter profile, as was popular during colonial years. Eighteenth-century portraits were meant to depict their subjects' occupations or special interests, and so Levy's finger points to the ship in the background, showing that he was a merchant. The dog across his lap shows his gentility and unity with nature. Portrait by Gerardus Duyckinck.

colonies. He owned ships that traded among England, the Caribbean, and the colonies. Active in the purchase of the first Jewish cemetery land in New York, he was a major contributor to the Jewish community; but he contributed to the Christian community, too, for he was one of five Jews who gave money for the completion of the spire of Trinity Church in New York. A portrait of Levy by Gerardus Duyckinck, now at the American Jewish Historical Society, shows a ship in the background, indicating his status as a merchant. It was typical of the paintings of the period to represent in the portrait the sitter's occupation and social status.

With greater freedom to participate in society than they had enjoyed in the old country, one would hope that the Jews in colonial times would not be faced with much prejudice or discrimination. Unfortunately that was not the case.

On August 28, 1655, Stuyvesant and the New Amsterdam Council resolved to exclude Jews from military service, so the right to defend their own city was denied to them. Along with the denial of this civic right came the imposition of a special city tax. This is an example of the struggle the Jews faced at every stage of their quest for equal rights and full citizenship. The resolution was challenged on November 5, 1655, by two Jewish citizens, Jacob Barsimson and Asser Levy. The council and director general said that the resolution would stand, and that if Barsimson and Levy felt this was injurious to them, they had the right to depart.

Eventually, the Constitution of the United States, adopted in 1787, granted equality, civil rights, and religious privileges to all citizens at the federal level; but not all of the states' constitutions provided these rights as well. Maryland's constitution, for example, stated that only Christians could hold public offices or commissions. In 1787, Solomon Etting, a Jewish merchant in Baltimore, unsuccessfully petitioned the General Assembly to grant Jews all the rights of citizenship. It took the assembly until 1826 to grant full equality to "the sect of people professing the Jewish religion." This bill, approved on the last day of the session in Maryland's General Assembly, became known as the "Jew Bill." In that year, both Solomon Etting and Jacob Cohen (1789–1869), were elected to the Baltimore City Council.

Even with all the anti-Semitism they encountered, the Jewish colonials still kept two basic goals in mind. The first was to live with and work alongside their Christian neighbors, whether in private business, community projects, or the development of a Jewish-Christian understanding and respect. The Reverend Ezra Stiles, who eventually became the President of Yale University, was overwhelmed with the learning he sought and received from the Jewish clergy at the Touro Synagogue in Newport, Rhode Island. In his correspondence with Touro's learned Jewish leaders, he often referred to the trading of ideas and values. He even commented on the beauty of the synagogue's edifice, the elegance of the service and liturgy and, most of all, on the hospitality he received at Touro and from the Jewish community in general.

The second goal was to contribute to the overall benefit of the general community. Jews took an active role in helping to secure social and religious rights, not only for themselves, but for all Americans. This was often seen in the Jewish support of the American Revolution and in the fight for independence. Francis Salvador, for example, was a young Jew of a prominent Spanish-Portuguese family. He became one of the most respected South Carolina plantation owners. The Salvador family had come from Europe with the seal of their important status, a coat of arms. Salvador became an early supporter of the patriots' cause and, in 1774, he was elected to represent his district in the First and Second Provincial Congresses in South Carolina. He was the first South Carolina Jew to be elected to an important public office usually occupied only by Christians. While inspecting upstate frontiers, he was murdered and scalped by Tory-led Indians, thus becoming the first Jew to give his life for the cause of American freedom in the Revolutionary War. Francis Salvador was hailed as a hero by George Washington, and today there is a memorial plaque behind the City Hall of Charleston commemorating his heroic deeds.

Another example of public service by Jewish Americans on behalf of their entire community was provided by Rebecca Gratz, the daughter of Michael and Miriam Gratz of Philadelphia. In 1801, together with her mother, Rebecca helped found the Female Association for Relief of Women and Children in Reduced Circumstances, which benefited the whole community of Philadelphia, secular as well as religious.

Each person featured in this book represents some contribution to America in the early years. Some of those contributions were made before the American Revolution in 1776; some during the Revolution; and some after that period. Most important, each of these people whether consciously or not, made a significant mark in America's early development. In one way or another, the Jewish Americans in this book are noteworthy for their good taste, and more importantly, for their good deeds.

Luis Moses Gomez

*The Oldest Jewish House
in America*

*Isaac Gomez, son of Luis Moses Gomez, patriarch
of the New York family. The family came from
Madrid, Spain, via France, and also had ties to
the Caribbean islands. Isaac was married on
the Dutch island of Curaçao. His son, Isaac Jr.,
married Abigail, the daughter of Aaron
Lopez of Newport, Rhode Island.*

LUIS Moses Gomez, the founder of one
of the most important families in eigh-
teenth- and nineteenth-century New York,
was born in Madrid in the 1660s, during the
Spanish Inquisition. His family were practicing Marranos—Jews who practiced their
religion secretly at home while outwardly
pretending to be Catholics. During that period in history, it was at best dangerous to be
known as a Jew, and Luis's family had to
endure all types of punishment.

According to the new Jewish Standard Encyclopedia, some of Luis's ancestors included Antonio Gomez, a professor of medicine at Coimbra in the 1580s
who was sentenced to death by the Inquisition in 1619 for being a Judaizer;
Antonio Enriquez de Paz (1600–1660), a popular playwright and poet in Spain
who, after being burned in effigy by the Inquisition in 1640, openly returned
to Judaism in Amsterdam; Diego Enriquez Basurto, his son, who was also a
poet and playwright; and Duarte Gomez (d. 1608), a martyr who came home
from Solonika to Portugal and taught his fellow Jews that Jewish people in
Portugal were in fact being burned at the stake by the auto-da-fé, as they had
been in Spain.

Luis's father, Isaac, was a nobleman, probably in Portugal. The Portuguese
king warned Isaac that times were going to get very difficult for people of Jewish descent. Isaac sent his son, Luis, and Luis's mother first to France to flee the
hands of the Inquisition and then to England. From England, Luis went
in 1703 to America, where he received a "Letter of Denization" from the

then-reigning monarch of England, Queen Anne, which allowed him to live in America with "all of the privileges of the most favorite subjects." These privileges included holding land in fee simple and holding both civil and military offices.

Luis was forty years old when he arrived in New York. He soon began to prosper in the import-export business. He was involved, for example, in the export of wheat as well as chintz, silk, and other fabrics. He also imported wines from Portugal. He purchased many city properties and became an investor in New York real estate. He was best known, however, as a trader of furs and pelts.

At age fifty-five, Luis purchased a tract of land in Marlboro, New York, in the Hudson River Valley wilderness. The local Dutch inhabitants referred to this property as the Dansk Commons, or "The Devil's Dance Chamber," because of the legends told by the local Indian tribes about their ancestors' ceremonies and dances.

Because of the proximity to the local Indian tribes, Luis decided to secure his property by building his house and store with as much protection as possible. He put the back of his house against a hillside, and he laid the foundation of his store on the top of a hill. He built the walls of local massive stones. His front door, a "Dutch door," could open either completely or only at the top, providing another form of protection.

Luis traded often with the local Algonquin Indians for the much-desired furs and pelts. In return, Luis gave the Indians the goods they wanted: utensils, beads, glass, trinkets, rum, and guns. The Indians also loved to look at and touch the silk fabrics Luis imported from England and Spain, and they often wore shirts of these fine materials. Luis also had other business ventures in the Hudson River Valley, including a lime business and a saw mill.

His home and store or trading post on the Hudson River is still intact today. It is the oldest structure still standing built by a Jew in America. Luis Gomez was the first president of the first synagogue in America, Shearith Israel. He also helped to purchase the site on Mill Street for Shearith Israel. (That synagogue is now in its fifth location, at Central Park West and Seventieth Streets.) He was also a contributor to Trinity Church in New York. He also helped to establish the Chatham Square Cemetery, the site of the earliest Jewish burials in New York. He himself is buried there. His tombstone, written in both English and Portuguese, bears the words, "The Venerable and Beloved Moses Gomez." When he died in 1750, his house and store were sold by his heirs.

*   *   *

The Gomez Mill House, built by Luis Moses Gomez in the Hudson River area of New York, is the oldest American Jewish residence still standing. Born in Spain, Luis Gomez was a founder of Shearith Israel Congregation. From his house and store, Gomez traded in furs and pelts.

Luis had six sons: Isaac, Benjamin, Jacob, Mordecai, Daniel, and David. Jacob was killed at sea in 1722 by members of a Spanish vessel, but the other five sons all became prominent and successful leaders in the Jewish community in eighteenth-century New York. Daniel Gomez was involved in trade with the West Indies. In the *New-York Gazette* of June 24, 1751, he advertised "A New Shipment from Liverpool of Cheshire Cheese, Loaf Sugar, Cutlery, Pewter, Grindstones, Coral, and Earthenware in Casks and Crates." Daniel also became a successful real estate developer.

Luis's grandson, Benjamin (1769–1828) was one of the first Jewish booksellers in North America.

One of the descendants of the Gomez family was Harmon Hendricks, who at the beginning of the nineteenth century was instrumental in bringing the copper industry from England to America for the first time. In the twentieth century, another descendant, Benjamin Cardoso, sat on the highest court in the land, the Supreme Court of the United States. Yet another was Emma Lazarus, whose poetry was so respected that her words are on the base of the Statue of Liberty in New York Harbor.

Give me your tired, your poor,
Your huddled masses yearning to breathe free,
The wretched refuse of your teeming shore.
Send these, the homeless, tempest-tost to me,
I lift my lamp beside the golden door.

To this day, the family and descendants of Luis Moses Gomez are still counted among the most prominent Jewish leaders in New York and of their beloved Shearith Israel.

Abigail Franks

She Challenged Her Jewish
Community to Reform

Abigail Franks, daughter of New York merchant Moses Levy. Abigail could read and write, and her many letters describe her life in eighteenth-century America and give her outspoken opinions on various subjects.

BORN Bilhah Abigail Levy in 1696 in London, Abigail Franks was one of the most outspoken women of her time.

She was raised in an affluent family. Her father, Moses Raphael Levy, born in Germany in 1665, came to New York from England in 1695. A successful merchant with a fleet of ships that sailed between the colonies, the Caribbean, England, and North Africa, he owned seventy acres of land in New York and was a very successful real estate investor. Abigail's mother was Richa Asher, Moses's first wife. When Richa died early in their marriage, Moses married Grace Mears. Moses fathered twelve children, seven with his second wife. Considered one of New York's wealthiest citizens at the time of his death in 1728, he was buried at Chatham Square in New York, in the oldest Jewish cemetery in America. His tombstone is well preserved and inscribed with these words in Hebrew, Spanish, and English: "O frail Adam, what the earth surely produces, Death by his power reduces thy heavenly part—man being fled. Alas, the other parts are dead."

Abigail's stepmother, who raised her, and her father were both active in establishing the Jewish community in New York and were contributors to the first synagogue on Mill Street in the area that is commonly referred to today as Wall Street. Still surviving today at its fifth location, the congregation is now known as Shearith Israel. The Levy family was also well known and highly respected in New York society at the time, even contributing financially to the completion of the spire of New York's famed Trinity Church. It was in

Shearith Israel, the first Jewish congregation in America, at its fifth location, in New York, in 1730. The synagogue today houses the "Little Synagogue" within its walls, containing parts of the original Mill Street building.

this spirit of participation in the various levels of life and society around them that Abigail was raised.

Abigail was most unusual for her time. In a day when a colonial woman was expected to be responsible only for the care of her house and children, Abigail Franks could read and write, and she did a great deal of both throughout her lifetime. Most of her writing was in the form of letters to family and friends. In the eighteenth century, letter writing was considered an art.

In 1712 she married Jacob Franks (1688–1769), a business apprentice to her father. Jacob had been born in Germany, the son of Naphtali Franks, a merchant, and had, as a young man, emigrated to London to seek his fortune as a writer. An intellectual who as a youth was the master of many languages as well as of Jewish law and who later earned a degree in divinity, Jacob thought that the English world had more to offer for his literary tastes. At some time, though, while still in England, Jacob decided that the road to wealth was better paved through commerce than through literature, and in 1708, he came to America as a merchant rather than as a writer.

Jacob was active in New York's Shearith Israel, and like his father-in-law he became an eminent merchant in New York, trading in tea, rice, guns, diamonds, and coral. He, too, is buried in Chatham Square Cemetery.

The Franks raised nine children. Abigail insisted on the best education for them. Their sons were taught at the most elite school in New York at the time, run by Alexander Malcolm. Since Abigail wanted her boys to have a classical

The Jews in Early America

education, they were taught Latin, geometry, science, music, and the arts. For practical reasons, they were also schooled in mercantile navigation, so they could at some future time assume the responsibilities of the family's business. The daughters were educated by tutors from the Shearith Israel Synagogue school. There they were taught English, art, and literature. Abigail was determined to have her girls receive as fine an education as her boys—a radical concept for the times.

Abigail was a woman of culture. Very intelligent, she had an extensive knowledge of English literature and the philosophers of the eighteenth-century Age of Enlightenment. In addition to books, she read newspapers, magazines, and pamphlets, and she encouraged her children in "the duty of reading and studying while they were still young and leisure was theirs." Abigail was a thinker, and what she thought she communicated to others. She knew she had the right to her thoughts, and, through her letters, the right to have her thoughts heard.

An observant Jew who adhered to religious dicta, Abigail was very proud of the

Jacob Franks, husband of Abigail Franks and a successful merchant. Jacob originally studied literature in England in order to become a writer, but decided that the pursuit of business would be more lucrative. He was also a scholar of the Old Testament.

fact that she never wrote on the Sabbath, observed all the holy days, kept a strict kosher home, and attended synagogue regularly. However she was often critical of her coreligionists and often skeptical of their rituals. She voiced her criticism about the members of her synagogue in letters to her children. She was not liked because she also voiced her opinions openly.

For example, in a letter of October 1739 to her son, Naphtali, a young merchant living in London, she confessed,

> I must own I can't help condemning the many superstitions we Jews are clogged with and heartily wish a Calvin or a Luther would rise among us, I answer for myself, I would be the first of their followers, for I don't think religion should consist only of idle ceremonies and works of supererogation, which if they send people to heaven, we and the Papists will have the greatest title to go there together.

With these words, Abigail characterizes Jewish religious practices as very superstitious and overceremonious, even comparing them with the practices of the Catholic Church. She particularly criticizes the religion's emphasis on heaven, which she felt should be secondary to lessons in dealing with the problems and realities of living here on earth. It is hard to imagine how inflammatory this kind of suggestion, had it been made public, might have been during colonial times.

In another letter, there is this criticism: "Jews have misconstrued the Book [of Mosaic Law] which imbues them with their very identity." We find that her concern here comes out of an angry ferment in her synagogue over the pending marriage of a Sephardic boy to an Ashkenazic girl. According to Abigail, who was herself Ashkenazic, the Portuguese or Sephardic Jews in New York thought of themselves as an elite. As a result they tended to keep to themselves and to look down on all the Ashkenazim. In her view, this hierarchical clash of customs was unacceptable and not in keeping with the Mosaic Laws. She suggested that to correct this thinking, a new form of philosophical as well as religious rationale was necessary. Abigail thought New York's Jews must better understand that Mosaic Laws did not intend there to be two Judaisms, but only one. Jews are equal in God's eyes, she believed, and if this equality was good enough for God, it should be good enough for us. Abigail believed that it would behoove the elders of her synagogue to restate Judaism's purpose for the congregation's reeducation if they could be so inclined.

In yet another example of Abigail's thoughts on the need for reform, she stated in a letter dated 20 December, 1741, "I don't often see any of our ladys but at synagogue." She detested the gossip she heard by the women in her synagogue. She knew that they were prejudiced against her, not just because she was an Ashkenazi Jew in a synagogue filled with Sephardic Jews, but because she spent her time differently from the way they spent theirs. Abigail read fine literature to enlighten her mind, and she wrote many letters to express her feelings. This was what Abigail did for herself, and the outspoken and challenging set of goals she proposed for the women of her congregation was typical of her comments on the social mores of her peers.

Abigail was a very complex person in her moods and desires, and even though she was critical of her Jewish community, she felt it was necessary to maintain ties to it. In this regard, she helped by contributing money for the building of the Shearith Israel structure and funds to keep it maintained. She attended synagogue even when she was not in the best of health. She had arthritis and she wore glasses as her eyesight began to fail her. Not only did Abigail take many medicines, she also took snuff, which she had her son Naphtali send to her from England.

Abigail also taught her children to share her love of beautiful objects. In another of her letters, she referred to a gift her son Naphtali and his wife Phila sent from England to his brother, David, on the occasion of David's marriage, a beautiful silver fruit bowl made in London by one of the most important English silversmiths of the time, Paul de Lamerie. On that bowl is the coat of arms of the Franks family, executed in 1733. This bowl is today in the collection of the Metropolitan Museum of Art, along with other Franks family pieces also made by de Lamerie, an elegant cake basket and a silver teakettle. All of these objects were typical of the best workmanship available at that time.

During the eighteenth century, it was common for families of the Franks's standing to have their portraits painted. The eleven family portraits of the Levy-Franks family, executed between 1725 and 1735, constitute the largest collection extant of a single American family executed by a single artist. The artist to whom these paintings are attributed was Gerardus Duyckinck. The style of this painting, which was very popular in England and in America, had been developed by Sir Godfrey Kneller of London, who had in turn learned his art from Frederick Bols, a young Dutch student of Rembrandt. The Dutch style of portraiture appealed to the colony of New Yorkers, who after all lived in a town originally settled by the Dutch. In her portraits, Abigail is pictured as quite plump and matronly. Her blue satin and lace dress is elegant and in the latest fashion of the period. This is also true of her swept-up coiffure and the light use of her makeup and jewelry.

The Franks family belonged to the upper class of Jewish society in New York, but because of her wealth, Abigail's social standing in the general New York society was assured as well, even though she thought of herself as primarily a devout and loyal Jew. She and her husband, Jacob, were often invited to dine with the important members of both the political and mercantile societies of the day.

There was a drawback, though, to being such a cosmopolitan and participating in the conversation and commerce of the public sphere. Such exposure could lead to "acculturation, assimilation, and integration of the Jews into the Protestant English culture of eighteenth-century New York," and that proved particularly troublesome for some of the mercantile elite, including the Franks family. For Abigail, it became especially painful when two of her children, Phila and David, both having been exposed to people of other religious backgrounds, married outside the Jewish faith.

Abigail's distress upon learning of her daughter Phila's marriage to Oliver Delancey, a British loyalist, is shown in a letter written to her son in 1743: "God what a shock it was when they acquainted me She had left the House to go to the house of a Delancey—since then my house and my thoughts have become my prison." Abigail didn't speak to her daughter or son-in-law for months after their elopement. In fact, Abigail didn't want to see anyone.

Her despondency arose from something more than Phila's disregard for her parents' wishes. This marriage entailed a flight from the Jewish identity Abigail so loved. Abigail believed that the family was the primary institution for preserving Jewish heritage in America. She also saw her son, David, of Philadelphia, for whom the beautiful silver was made, marry Margaret Evans, a Gentile. Another daughter, Richa, never married at all, rather than marry her Episcopalian lover and break her mother's heart once again.

Abigail's distress at the intermarriages of two of her children proved justified over the course of time. Every one of her great-grandchildren would eventually be baptized a Christian. By the beginning of the nineteenth century, none of the Franks were Jewish.

Abigail Franks did leave a legacy of loyalty to her Judaism, however, which was expressed in her financial support of her synagogue. Because she and her husband, Jacob, donated the funds to lay one of the cornerstones of the 1733 building, they are among those founding members still honored today, on the seventh day of Passover and the first day of Rosh Hashanah each year at the holiday services, when their names are lovingly read aloud to the congregation.

And of course for Abigail's personal legacy, there are her thoughts passed on through her letters. Thirty-seven letters still attest to her outspoken and often critical attempts to have the Jewish community around her change their ways from what she called "inane and superstitious to a more educated and genteel." Her sharp eye for detail in these letters still gives us an important perspective on Jews in New York during colonial times that can be found nowhere else.

Abigail Franks died in 1756. Her rare and unusual view of family and social life, through her wit, irritations, interests, and her often frank constructive criticisms, add significantly to our knowledge of Jewish history in America in the eighteenth century. Perhaps most of all, Abigail will be remembered for saying to her Jewish community: "Reform."

David and Richa Franks, two of Abigail and Jacob's children. David married a Christian, Margaret Evans, and moved to a house called Woodford in Fairmont Park, Philadelphia. Richa preferred never to marry at all rather than marry her Christian lover, which would have broken her mother's heart once again.

Myer Myers

*A Thing of Beauty
Is a Joy Forever*

Sugar bowl by Myer Myers, circa 1760, engraved with the name of its owner, AH VAN DEURSEN. *The shape of this bowl is one of the most popular American forms. The top rim and foot are gadrooned.*

AMONG the most famous of the early American gold and silversmiths was Myer Myers. He is considered the first native-born Jewish-American craftsman. A contemporary of silversmith Paul Revere, Myers was born in 1723 in New York, the eldest of seven children—three sons and four daughters. His parents, Solomon and Judith, both emigrants from England, became citizens of New York in 1723 when the reversal of an old British law for the first time allowed the naturalization of Jews in the New York Colony. Until that time, Jews had not been permitted to hold the important title of citizen, but were referred to only as residents.

Solomon, Myer's father, had a small shop in New York, although records are not specific enough to tell what products he sold. From what we do know about him, it's possible that this shop did not provide the Myers family with enough income to feed seven children, for in 1728, Solomon was also listed as a working custodian at his synagogue in New York, Shearith Israel, to supplement the family's income.

Solomon and Judith Myers had joined Shearith Israel shortly after arriving in New York and quickly became involved in its affairs. We know this because the synagogue's records list Solomon Myers as a contributor of twelve shillings for the synagogue's Chatham Square Cemetery. Solomon Myers must have had a good relationship with Shearith Israel, because it was noted in the synagogue's papers that after his death in October 1743, the congregation alotted his family thirty pounds a year, as well as their supply of Passover bread and eight cords of wood. In colonial times, all of the Pesach bread was baked and provided by the synagogues.

It is quite likely that Myer Myers received a good part of his education at the Shearith Israel school, as the opportunity was typically offered to the children of the families of the congregation. That education was supplemented by a seven-year apprenticeship starting at age twelve to an unknown master. Myers established his first shop at the Meal Market, a part of the lower end of what we today call Wall Street in New York. His outstanding career as a colonial silversmith was to span fifty productive and creative years.

Myer Myers was married twice. His first wife, Elkalah Cohen Myers, died in August, 1765 at the age of thirty after bearing five children, one of whom did not survive infancy. Not long afterwards, in March 1767, Myers married again, this time to Joyce Mears, of a very well-respected New York Jewish family. Joyce and Myer bore eight children, three of whom died in infancy. (The mortality rate of children in colonial times was very high.) Joyce's sister, Caty, was the wife of Myer's younger brother, Asher Myers.

Myer Myers is best remembered as one of the most important and successful silversmiths of his time. Starting in his first shop and continuing throughout his career, he fashioned a variety of silver objects for his many clients, some of whom were prominent citizens and prosperous colonial merchants who emulated the life styles of their English cousins across the sea, acquiring silver for pleasure as well as for its utility. For example, he created a salver or tray for the New York merchant David Grimes in the Rococo style, which is now housed at the New York Historical Society. In 1760 he fashioned a mustard pot; mustard was used by the English to flavor meats, fish, and potatoes, much as we use catsup today.

Among the many beautiful silver pieces made by Myer Myers and now in public and private collections are a caster or container used to hold sugar or cinnamon, its elegant design of the typically Dutch Bulbous shape; a pair of wine casters with the crest of the Schuyler family of New York, which uses a delicate filigree design typical of the best work done by silversmiths of this period; and a candle snuffer and tray made for John and Catherine Livingstone Reade. Besides the work that Myers did for the secular community, there are many fine pieces of silver that he made for individual colonial Jewish families: a beaker or cup made for Reyna and Isaac Moses of New York; a circumcision set made for Isaac Seixas of New York in 1762; and a salver or small tray made in 1765 for David and Margaret Evans Franks of Philadelphia.

Myers catered to an ever-increasing patronage of wealthy colonial merchants and tradesmen who in the absence of banks frequently invested the family wealth in expensive silver *objets d'art*. Colonists also invested in silver rather than in stocks and bonds owing to the unsettled condition of the many markets during that period. Hence, clever designers like Myer Myers became important in the business world, filling a role not unlike that of investment brokers. For example, he made a sauce pot for Lord Loudon of England, who commanded a regiment for the British during the Revolutionary War, that was clearly made as an investment as well as for utility, according to a piece of correspondence accompanying it.

In addition to "domestic ware," or silver made especially for an individual's personal use (or investment) Myers also created "ecclesiastical ware," also referred to as "ceremonial plate," for synagogues and churches. For example, he made an alms bowl, a bowl for donations to the poor, for the Forty-First Presbyterian Church in New York City. Done in the Early Mid-Century Style (1740–1760), it has simple straight sides and rim. It is now preserved at the Metropolitan Museum of Art in New York City. He made a set of Rimmonim or scroll bells that sits on top of the Torah for Philadelphia's Mikveh Israel Congregation in 1772. He made a baptismal bowl for the Brick Presbyterian Church in New York City.

Myers was considered a master of ongoing stylistic change throughout his career, as his work progressed through three distinct periods in eighteenth century design, the Early Mid-Century (1740–1760); the Classical or Rococo Period (1760–1790); and the Federal Period (1790–1810). But although Myers's productions were often inspired by English prototypes and their basic style and form of decoration were typical of trends of the time, Myers also displayed a remarkable sense of creative design, and his creations often were characterized by his own fine line and proportion.

This individual creativity is especially evident in Myers's spoons, for which he is justly famous. (To attract his clients, Myers was known to have advertised in the newspapers and handbills of the day. In one advertisement of 1768, there are these words, "New fashioned spoons feathered on the handles.") Myers made spoons that show his work could be characteristically quite simple, graceful, and sturdy. Some long spoons with long bowls were used for extracting marrow from lamb and beef bones, considered a delicacy in colonial times. Myers made other types of silver spoons as well, which show the types of food eaten in America at this period of time. These included a toddy spoon for mixing hot drinks or liquor usually drunk at bedtime (now in the Clearwater collection at the Metropolitan Museum of Art), and a ladle for soups, stews, or punch for Nathan and Susan McIntosh Smith of Massachusetts.

Sterling silver Rimmonim *to go on the tops of Torah scrolls, by Myer Myers. Myers made* Rimmonim *like these for the congregations of Shearith Israel in New York, Touro Synagogue in Newport, and Mikveh Israel in Philadelphia.*

Above: The sterling silver spoon by Myer Myers bears the popular feather-edged pattern. Its bowl is of the sort used for desserts such as puddings and pies.

Below: The back of the spoon shown above, showing how Myers signed his work in full. He also often used his initials, MM.

For a silversmith, one of the important decisions to make is how to mark his work. Although Myers used his own initials conjoined in a rectangle at one point, and separated in a sloped cartouche at another time, the maker's mark he seems to have preferred consisted of his name written on the back of the piece in script. The greatest number of pieces of Myers's forms known to exist appear to have been marked in this fashion.

Myers also chose to use a molded silver shell as often as possible in his designs. He used shells on the rims of silver trays and on the tops and bases of candlesticks, as decoration. He even used a shell motif as an affixitive. Affixitives are the places where one part of a piece, such as a leg or a handle, is attached to the body of the piece.

It is interesting to note that in executing his work, Myers occasionally needed to depend on the work of other New York manufacturers as well. For example he purchased copper from the Uriah Hendricks family, the Jewish family that had introduced the manufacturing of copper to America for the first time. Copper was often used as a base for Myers's silver objects or as an additional strengthening to the silver compound itself. And from the Hendricks's papers, it is known that Myers fashioned the copper handles for much of the Hendricks's personal collection of furniture.

Another craftsman with whom Myers worked was Mr. Joshua Delapleine, a well-known New York–based cabinet maker. Mr. Delapleine supplied the wooden handles for some of Myers's silver coffee and tea pots. And in return, Mr. Delapleine hired Myers to create the handles for many of his funeral caskets. As a cabinet maker, Delapleine was often called upon to provide the wooden caskets for his patrons, including those for the Hendricks family and some of their servants.

During the height of his career, a period of intense output of incredibly beautiful silver pieces, Myers also was busy pursuing the other interests of his life, including land speculations. Following the Treaty of Paris in 1761, the province of New Hampshire made more than a hundred land grants available in what is now the state of Vermont. Myers was one of the citizens who was granted land in the "Underhill and Westford township." Myers, it seems, never had any intention of settling on this property; he merely used it as an investment. He also, along with his partner and friend, Michael Gratz, a well-known merchant from Philadelphia, purchased a tract of land in Woodbury, Littlefield County, Connecticut.

Myers both invested and sought investors in the Spruce Hill Lead Mine also lying in the County of Littlefield, Connecticut. On November 27, 1765, he issued a contract to Michael Gratz, wherein Mr. Gratz promised to pay forty-five pounds, six shillings and sixpence for one-sixteenth of the Spruce Hill Lead Mine. In return, Myers promised to give him a sufficient title for the same piece.

Along with Myers's interest in land speculation, his participation in Masonry also reflected his growing status in his community. He had become a Mason in 1746 as a young man. Now prosperous, in 1769, Myers was named the Senior Warden of his lodge, serving under another well-known colonial Jew, Moses Michael Hays. Hays at that time was the master of the King David Lodge in New York City. Both Myers and Hays were dedicated Masons in New York until the beginning of the British occupation of New York during the Revolutionary War, at which point Hays moved the Lodge, first to Newport where he resided for a short time and then to Boston, where it continues to this day. In Boston, one of Hays's fellow Lodge members was another famous silversmith, Paul Revere. It was for Moses Michael Hays that Paul Revere made the only silver he ever executed for a Jewish client. Those pieces of silver, including teaspoons and a teapot made for Moses Michael Hays—are still in existence today. The teapot is at the Museum of Fine Arts in Boston, and the teaspoons are in the collection of the State Department in Washington, D.C.

The story of this Paul Revere silver is especially interesting, because Moses Michael Hays had some of that silver made as wedding presents for two of his own daughters, both of whom moved to Richmond, Virginia when they married two of Moses Myers's sons. These offspring of Hays and Myers helped begin the Jewish community in Richmond, and helped form the Richmond synagogue, Beth Shalome (now called Beth Ahaba), in 1785. Some of their descendants still live in Virginia, where many preserved objects connected with the Myers family exist as well.

Besides being a silversmith, a Mason, a businessman, and a family man, Myers was a Jew who felt a strong responsibility to the Jewish community. Even as a young apprentice in 1743, he was listed independently from his family as a donor of three shillings to the Shearith Israel Synagogue fund. At age twenty-one, he was asked by the synagogue's board of trustees to represent the synagogue as a witness to the will of one of its members, Joshua Isaacs, a prominent New York merchant. This request was quite an honor for such a young man, and it indicates the high regard with which Myers was recognized by his Jewish community.

And that was only the beginning, because service to his synagogue became Myers's lifelong commitment. His beloved Shearith Israel Congregation was a woven part of the fabric of his life, and that devotion led to many and various responsibilities he assumed on behalf of this devotion. Myers was chosen at one time to be a member of an important school committee, appointed by the Shearith Israel Board of Trustees to inspect the congregation's educational system and to report on the progress of its students. It is not known exactly how he went about this task, but it is known that its results were formally issued in writing. Myers also served as vice president and then as president of the synagogue starting in 1759. He actually assumed this role for two terms, judging by the records still in existence indicating his positions.

In 1770, Myers headed up a fund-raising committee to secure the money needed to help continue the building of the Newport synagogue, Touro. This synagogue, designed by the famed colonial architect Peter Harrison, was dedicated in 1763. During the colonial period, it was not unusual for one congregation to help another congregation in need. This often happened between the five colonial congregations, as well as the Jewish communities of the Caribbean, England, and Holland.

Myers was to have another connection to the Newport community as well, for he was hired to make the Rimmonim, or tops of Torahs symbols, just as he is presumed to have done for his own Shearith Israel.

Because of Myers's relationship with Shearith Israel, it was long believed that he had contributed the pair of Rimmonim to his own congregation. However, that wasn't the case; the congregation's records reveal that in 1765 and 1770, respectively, thirty-six pounds, four shillings and thirty-nine pounds, ten shillings were paid to Myer Myers for Rimmonim. There are also notations of other silver items made to order by Myers and paid for by Shearith Israel: a pair of candlesticks and a pitcher and bowl used to wash hands, both made for the burial society. All of this information indicates he was able to keep his synagogue activities separate from those of his professional life.

By the year 1775, the American colonies' struggle for liberty had finally resolved itself into an organization for war. Like most of the Jews in the colonies at that time, Myers was in total agreement with the need to break away from Great Britain. Having taken that stand forced Myers and his family to flee New York along with other members of his congregation when the British entered New York in 1777. The Myers family went first to Connecticut, where he is believed to have organized a campaign to have members of the various general colonial communities remove the lead sashes from their windows and replace them with wood. He then helped melt the lead from these sashes and molded it into cannon balls and bullets for the colonials to use against the British. It is unclear whether or not he received any pay for this service.

During his stay in Connecticut, Myers overheard a neighbor speak openly of treasonous activity against the colonial forces. Incensed by this information, he wrote to the authorities about the offender. It is not hard to imagine how angry he must have been to take such an action.

In 1782 the Myers family moved from Connecticut to Philadelphia. There they became actively involved with Philadelphia's Mikveh Israel Synagogue. Myers contributed twelve guineas to that congregation. Myers was hardly a stranger to the Philadelphia congregation, having supplied the Rimmonim for their Torah tops. He had also made many objects for individual Jewish patrons in Philadelphia as well. For example, he made a silver ginger jar, copied from a Chinese porcelain form, for the Michael Gratz family about 1760. Myers also made a silver seal for the David Franks family of Philadelphia. Often these seals were used as memorials to a family member or to honor a particular occasion such as a wedding. And anything made in silver, even a seal, was another way to bank the family's wealth.

The Myers family stayed in Philadelphia until the end of the Revolutionary War, when they moved back to New York. In 1787, Myers reopened his shop, this time at 29 Princess Street at the corner of Broad, in what was known at that time as the Federal Hall area. It was an important part of town and Myers was in good company as Federal Hall served then as the first capitol building of the United States.

Myer Myers was now sixty-three years of age and about to be recognized formally for the three most important activities of his life.

Within the field of his profession, Myers was given the honor of serving as the chairman of the New York Gold and Silver Society. The most important organization of its kind in America, this society was the closest thing America had to the well-known and respected gold and silver guilds of England and Europe. The position Myers was given in the society demonstrated how very much both he and his workmanship were appreciated by his peers.

Myers was also honored by the members of Shearith Israel congregation at about the same time. He was asked to serve as a representative from the Jewish community to George Clinton, the new Governor of New York. In this official capacity he delivered a letter to the governor welcoming him on behalf of the Jewish community. This obviously pleasurable assignment was the congregation's way of showing its appreciation for all he had done for Shearith Israel over the years.

The third honor came in 1790, when the first census in the United States listed Myer Myers as the titular head of the entire Myers household. For Myers, a devoted husband and father to this family, the listing of his name in this role was indeed a well-earned honor.

*   *   *

Early silver tankard by Myer Myers, circa 1760, with openwork scroll thumbpiece. Myers was president of the Gold and Silver Society of New York, the closest equivalent to the silver guilds of England. He was one of the most famous of New York's early silversmiths. Note the cover with a coin. The handle is engraved G/RN.

In 1795, at the age of seventy-two, Myer Myers died. A master of stylistic change throughout his fifty-year career, he will long be remembered for a large variety of beautiful objects. Examples of Myers's silver can be found in almost all the important museums of this country as well as in many private collections. The Yale Center of Art in New Haven, Connecticut, the Museum of the City of New York, and the Metropolitan Museum each have examples of his work wrought in gold as well as in silver. There is a gold shoe buckle now at the Yale Museum of Art, and a gold mourning ring made in 1764 is in the Museum of the City of New York. Some of the Myers silver is still in the possession of the descendants of the original owners.

Myers left behind him a reputation for superb workmanship. The superior quality of his work brought him many distinguished customers during his lifetime. Today, his work is prized for its craftsmanship as well as for its rarity. In the fifty years that he worked, his style evolved with the changing fashion, but his designs never varied in their excellence. He plied his craft with both success and honor. It is not hard to see why his work was so highly respected while he lived, and why it is today so highly coveted and prized.

Myers also lived as a useful and public-spirited citizen. He felt a responsibility to his fellow man. As a devoted member of his Jewish community, he was buried in the Spanish-Portuguese Cemetery fronting St. James Place on Chatham Square. Every year, Myers is honored as a Revolutionary War patriot at the Memorial Day service held at Chatham Square by present members of New York's Shearith Israel Synagogue. And even after his death, his family continued to pay his pledges to his congregation, according to the synagogue's historical account books and records.

If "A thing of beauty is a joy forever," then indeed we will always be grateful, and joyful, for both the life and the work of American colonial silversmith Myer Myers.

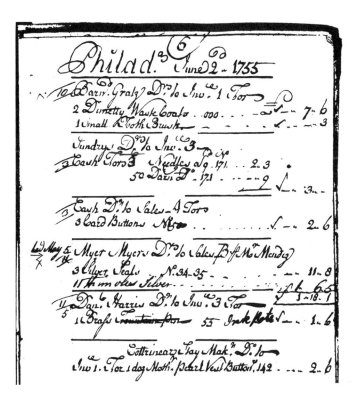

This excerpt from the daybook of the Philadelphia synagogue shows Myer Myers's name. Myers left New York during the Revolutionary War, when the British entered the city, and went to Philadelphia, a safer place to be. He made the silver Rimmonim for the Mikveh Israel congregation and was one of its founding contributors.

The Touro Synagogue of Newport

The Oldest Standing Synagogue in America

Interior of Touro Synagogue, showing the Sephardic style with the reader's desk or tevah in the middle of the room. All of this synagogue dates back to its founding by the Isaac Touro family.

NEWPORT, Rhode Island, was the first New England town to be settled by Spanish-Portuguese Jews. This happened in 1660, when fifteen Sephardic Jewish families arrived there from Holland. They chose Newport at least partly because the colony of Rhode Island had been founded with a philosophy of religious tolerance. Roger Williams, the governor, had left Massachusetts to form a more liberal community that would welcome all religions. He proclaimed that in his colony "Jewish population should have the right to practice their Judaism without molestation of governing body." He said that Jews could be "law-abiding citizens."

It took another hundred years, however, for those original fifteen families to develop into what could be called a well-established Jewish community. During that period, they met to worship in private homes. But in 1763, they established a center for their Sephardic congregation, which they called Yeshuat Israel. Today it is known as Touro Synagogue.

By this time Newport was a bustling seaport, its harbor hosting many merchant ships carrying goods and foodstuffs from all over the world, including ships owned by several prosperous Newport Jews: Isaac and Nephtali Hart, Jacob Rodriguez Rivera, and Samuel and Aaron Lopez. All of these successful men were supporters of the new congregation.

Jacob Rodriguez Rivera was an important trader and merchant of spermaceti products, including candles made from whale oil, and he owned many pieces of property in Newport. His home was one of the most beautiful in

Exterior of Touro Synagogue, Newport, Rhode Island, whose cornerstone was laid in 1759. Its architect, Peter Harrison, had studied the work of Sir Christopher Wren in England. Touro is the oldest synagogue in America that is still in its original location.

Newport, and it has been preserved (although for another use) and can still be seen today. Aaron Lopez was another important property owner and one of the wealthiest men in all of the colonies. Known as "The Merchant Prince," he gained his wealth by trading in sugar, rum, building supplies, and, sadly, slaves.

Both of these men had roots in Spanish-Portuguese history, as did others in the community, and so they wanted their new synagogue Yeshuat Israel to be true to their tradition and to bespeak the importance of their heritage. Perched up on a hill, it was as imposing in the eighteenth century for its architectural elegance both inside and outside as were its parent synagogues in London and Amsterdam. It was designed by the famous Newport architect, Peter Harrison, who had trained in the style of the English architect, Sir

Christopher Wren. Peter Harrison's reputation as the designer of both the Redwood Library in Newport and the Trinity Church in Boston led to his preeminence in his field and certainly was the main reason the Jewish community chose him to create their house of worship.

One of the most influential leaders in the early years of the Newport synagogue was the Reverend Isaac Touro, who came to Newport in his twenties about 1758 and served the congregation there for more than twenty years. He became the hazzan or cantor of Yeshuat Israel Synagogue in 1763. He was married to Reyna, the sister of another well-known Jew during the colonial period in New England, Moses Michael Hays, one of the founders of the Bank of Boston. Reyna and Isaac had three children, Abraham, Judah, and Rebecca. Abraham and Judah never married; their sister, Rebecca, married Joshua Lopez.

During the time that Isaac Touro was the cantor in Newport, he became a friend to Dr. Ezra Stiles, who later became the President of Yale University. The two men would discuss Biblical meanings and the Hebrew language. Dr. Stiles left letters that stated just how impressed he was with the Jews of Newport, their beautiful synagogue, and all of the learning he received from the Reverend Touro.

During the American Revolution, the British occupied Newport. Most of the Jewish population, who were not loyal to the British Crown, departed. Isaac Touro also left at this time, first for New York and then for Kingston, Jamaica. He died in Jamaica at the age of forty-six in 1783.

After the Revolution, the decline of the Jewish population in Newport caused the closure of the synagogue there. If it hadn't been for the generosity of two men, the Reverend Isaac Touro's sons, Abraham and Judah Touro, the beautiful edifice in Newport might not be standing today.

Both Abraham and Judah were wealthy merchants and both felt a strong attachment to their father's synagogue. As a result, both men left considerable amounts of money in their wills for the preservation and general ongoing repair of the synagogue's building.

Abraham was the first brother to die, and in his will, which was dated March 4, 1822, he left ten thousand dollars to the "Legislature of the State of Rhode Island for the Purpose of Supporting the Jewish Synagogue in that State, Together with the Municipal Authority of the Town of Newport." He also left five thousand dollars to the town of Newport for repairing and preserving the street on which the synagogue stands. The town council of Newport then renamed that street Touro Street. Rebecca, Abraham's sister, saw to it that her brother's wishes for the synagogue's restoration be accomplished.

Judah Touro, son of Rabbi Isaac Touro, founder of the Touro Synagogue. Judah was a merchant in New Orleans, and became a major contributor to both Jewish and non-Jewish organizations, including other Hebrew congregations, schools, orphanages, hospitals, and organizations in the Holy Land.

Thirty-two years later, when his brother, Judah Touro, died, his will included a bequest of ten thousand dollars to the City of Newport, "For payment of a reader or minister to officiate in the Newport Synagogue." He also left funds to build a gateway for the old Jewish cemetery in Newport and to help repair the cemetery's walls and land. The money Judah left came to be known as the "Touro Jewish Synagogue Fund" which may help to explain the name change from Yeshuat Israel to Touro Synagogue.

But his story doesn't end there. In 1854, when Judah died, he had been living in New Orleans, Louisiana. While there, he built office buildings and a hospital, as well as a synagogue and an infirmary for the poor members of the community. In his will, he also left over five hundred thousand dollars for Catholic, Protestant, and other Jewish charities, including a number of Jewish synagogues in America. Judah's will shows the immense scope of his ability to give on a non-sectarian basis. It was said at his funeral that he was "a friend to the whole human race" and "that he was truly a man of universal philanthropy." According to Bernard Kusinitz, the late archivist of Touro Synagogue, "He may well be considered America's first real philanthropist."

Although Judah Touro died in New Orleans, his body was brought back to Newport to be buried in the Colonial Cemetery.

Thanks to the generosity of these two brothers, and thanks to their loyal respect for their father, Reverend Isaac Touro, the beautiful Spanish-Portuguese Touro Synagogue was rescued from closure and the building has been preserved to this day. Built in 1763, and still in use in its original location and structure, this synagogue has the distinction of being the oldest standing synagogue in America. Today Touro Synagogue is administered with the help of Congregation Shearith Israel in New York, which purchased the building and the property after the Revolution.

The burial grounds at Touro Synagogue, containing the gravestones of the Touro family, Moses Michael Hays, Jacob Rodriguez Rivera, and Aaron Lopez. It is well maintained, and can be visited today.

The Rivera–Lopez Family of Newport

From Marranos to Prominent Merchants

Jacob Rodriguez Rivera. A merchant, Rodriguez came from his birthplace in Portugal to Newport, Rhode Island, where he and his partner, John Brown (of the Brown University family in Providence), dealt in the production of spermaceti, used as fuel for oil lamps.

THIS chapter concerns two cousins, Jacob Rodriguez Rivera and Aaron Lopez, both born in Portugal in the early 1700s. Because these cousins were Jewish, and because the Inquisition was still going on at that time, they were not allowed to practice their religion. Instead, they were expected to live publicly as Catholics. Those who continued to practice Judaism did so secretly, in the privacy of their homes. These secret Jews were known as "Marranos," the Spanish word for "pigs."

Both men found this situation intolerable, and they both emigrated to America and settled in Newport, Rhode Island, where Jews had lived safely since 1660. There they could practice their religion publicly and proudly, and they soon became prominent members of the Jewish community, both for their success in business and for their contributions to and participation in the Touro Synagogue. In time Jacob Rodriguez Rivera and Aaron Lopez, already related by blood, became business partners, and then became related by marriage, thus uniting two very prominent, wealthy, and successful families.

Jacob Rodriguez Rivera, who became known as a merchant and a trader, introduced to America the manufacture of sperm oil, a trade he had learned in Portugal. Called spermaceti, this extract of whale oil was processed into a product used for oil lamps and the manufacture of candles. With the introduction of this industry, America became involved in the whaling industry, an industry that would help to support the New England states economically from 1750 to 1850. Seventeen factories were established to produce spermaceti products, and Newport was the seat of this successful industry until the beginning of the American Revolution. Jacob Rodriguez Rivera became a business partner in spermaceti products to men such as Nicholas Brown of Providence, Rhode Island. There are many letters which indicate the successful business transactions that were completed in the Brown–Rodriguez Rivera names. For example, there is a letter dated April 2, 1773 about "the necessity of uniting the whole body of spermaceti factories in order to control prices." This letter was written by Rodriguez Rivera to the Nicholas Brown Company.

Jacob Rodriguez Rivera was also involved in the mercantile industry, with investments in ships that brought cargo in the triangular trade between America, the West Indies, and Africa. There is an invoice dated January 10, 1770 which lists some of the merchandise brought in the ship *Cleopatra,* including such items as soap, flour, pine boards, fish, pork, lamp oil, and one hundred boxes of spermaceti candles. Rodriguez Rivera also shipped loads of rum, sugar, and—again, unfortunately—slaves.

Jacob Rodriguez Rivera was a major contributor to the building of the Newport Yeshuat Israel–Touro synagogue. Because of the money he contributed, Rodriguez Rivera laid one of the cornerstones of this edifice. Rodriguez Rivera owned many pieces of property in Newport. In 1770, Gilbert Stuart, the famous American portraitist, painted a portrait of Rodriguez Rivera, which is housed today at the Redwood Library, in Newport.

In 1777, during the American Revolution, Jacob Rodriguez Rivera, along with his wife, Hannah, and family, departed for safer ground. He found it in Boston and Leicester, Massachusetts. It is recorded in his papers that Rodriguez Rivera had six slaves and several servants who accompanied him to Leicester. We may assume that he chose Leicester because his daughter was already living there with her husband. (We will meet them later in this story.) At any rate, Rodriguez Rivera took up farming, a profession he was totally unfamiliar with. Although farming kept him busy, he longed to return to Newport and to the life of a merchant. Jacob had married his wife, Hannah Pimental Sassportas, on the Caribbean island of Curaçao, and then they moved to Newport.

Jacob's cousin, Aaron Lopez, was born in Portugal in 1731. As a Marrano, he was also denied the rights to practice Judaism openly. In Portugal, his name had been not Aaron, but Duarte. He married his first wife, Anna, in Portugal. They had a daughter, Catherine. In 1752, at age twenty-one, Aaron moved himself and his family to New York and then to Newport, Rhode Island where

Circumcision set used at the Brit Milah or Bris to fulfill the first Jewish covenant between a man and God. This is the type of set that would have been used to circumcise both Jacob Rodriguez Rivera and Aaron Lopez when they came to Newport, both having been denied their rights as Jews by the Inquisition in Portugal.

they not only began to practice Judaism openly but also returned to using their Hebrew names. Duarte became Aaron, his wife Anna became Abigail, and his daughter Catherine became Sarah. Abigail and Aaron were remarried in the Jewish tradition and Aaron, as an adult, was finally able to be circumcised.

Aaron's brother, Moses Lopez, known in Portugal as José Lopez, came to Newport with Aaron, and they became business associates, as well. The Lopez brothers already had other cousins in America, who helped them get started economically. One of his cousins was from the well-established Gomez family of New York. Daniel Gomez, the son of Luis Moses Gomez, was a merchant who helped build New York's first synagogue, Shearith Israel. He dealt in furs

Aaron Lopez, known as a "merchant prince" in America. Lopez was active in the Caribbean, bringing sugar, rum, and molasses as well as slaves on his ships. When the Rhode Island Colony denied citizenship to Jews, he became a naturalized citizen of the Colony of Massachusetts.

and pelts and was already wealthy by the time the Lopez family arrived in America. The Gomez–Lopez connection facilitated numerous business transactions. In time Aaron became known as a merchant prince, and was one of the wealthiest merchants in all of America. His business relations included a profitable partnership with his cousin and father-in-law, Jacob Rodriguez Rivera.

In 1761, Aaron Lopez requested from the colony of Rhode Island the right to become a naturalized citizen under the British Plantation Act of 1740. His petition was denied. Undismayed, Aaron Lopez did not give up the quest. In 1762, he moved to Swansea, Massachusetts, where he applied for naturalization again under the British Plantation Act of 1740. In Massachusetts, his naturalization was granted. Lopez also built a store for the goods he imported adjacent to his house in Leicester, Massachusetts. That building eventually became a school, the Leicester Academy.

His first wife, Abigail (Anna) died in 1762, in childbirth. She had already borne him eight children. Shortly thereafter, Aaron married again—this time to Sally (Sarah) Rodriguez, the daughter of his business partner and cousin, Jacob Rodriguez Rivera. His partner thus became his father-in-law. Aaron and Sarah had nine children. A portrait of Sarah with her son Joshua, also painted by Gilbert Stuart, is today at the Detroit Institute of Arts.

Like his father-in-law, Aaron Lopez engaged in a triangle trade between America, the West Indies, and Africa. On one of his ships, the *Hope,* Lopez brought goods consisting of looking glasses (mirrors), articles of clothing, hats and shoes, glass bottles, cotton, chocolate, wax, molasses, sugar, silk, pewter, Dutch tea, spermaceti products, and slaves. Lopez was regrettably involved in the slave trade in Guinea, Africa.

Aaron Lopez was known as a man of considerable wealth. His reputation as a merchant both in America, in England, and in Europe was considered impeccable. Today, there are receipts still in existence, that attest to his successful business prowess. He followed through on the economic growth of large profits at every opportunity. Known throughout the colonies, Lopez was to provide many ships' worth of cargo to his friend, Isaac de Costa of Charleston, South Carolina, who had come from England in 1742 as part of a very wealthy family.

Lopez was also known as a very generous, hospitable, and honest man. For example, he donated lumber to the Rhode Island College, founded by one of his business associates, the Nicholas Brown Company. Today the Rhode Island College is known as Brown University. Aaron also donated large funds of money to the Newport Touro Synagogue and he laid one of its cornerstones. Like many other Jewish residents of Newport, Aaron Lopez also donated

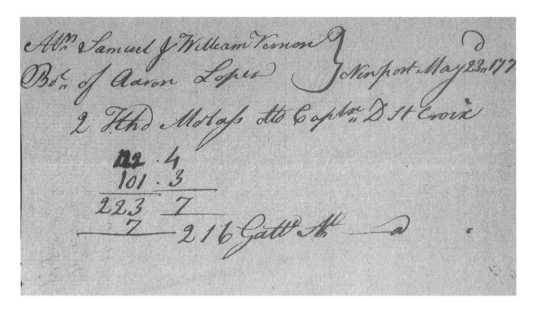

A bill of sale to Aaron Lopez of molasses from the Danish island of St. Croix—typical of the many bills Lopez kept in his accounting. Lopez was known throughout the colonies to be a very honest and trustworthy businessman.

generously to a campaign to raise money for the Jews in the Holy Land, sponsored by Rabbi Hyam Carigal from Palestine.

Aaron Lopez built a beautiful house in Newport in 1770 on Thames Street. His style of living included filling his house with beautiful furniture and keeping very beautiful silver on his table to serve his guests. He also kept his Jewish traditions, including not transacting any business on the Sabbath. He also helped to purchase for Touro Synagogue the silver Rimmonim or bells for the tops of the Torah made by the well-known Jewish-American silversmith, Myer Myers.

It is clear that although Aaron Lopez had a residence in Leicester, Massachusetts, he also considered Newport, Rhode Island his home. It is ironically fitting, then, that he died while traveling between the two homes, by drowning in a river on the road between Leicester and Newport, in 1782.

He was eulogized by the Reverend Ezra Stiles of Yale University in New Haven, Connecticut. That sermon, printed in the *Salem Gazette* in Salem, Massachusetts in 1782 called Lopez "a man of loyalty, generosity, and benevolence. He was an invaluable man to hundreds of distressed families as he exhibited always a point of view of perfection in the cardinal virtues that can adorn the human soul."

Aaron Lopez was buried at the Jewish Cemetery in Newport, Rhode

Island. His tombstone, like those of the most important men of a community, is in the form of an obelisk. He was outlived by his wife, Sarah, and by her father, Jacob Rodriguez Rivera, who was also his cousin, his business partner, his neighbor, and his father-in-law.

When he died in 1789, Jacob Rodriguez Rivera left to his son Abraham his five books of Moses on parchment, called the Torah, including the silver bells or Rimmonim for the tops of hisTorahs. He also gave his son a silver coffee pot, his sword, and all of his other books, wearing apparel, and all other gold and silver he possessed. He asked that his son support and maintain his aged brother, Isaac Rodriguez Rivera. He then divided the rest of his estate among Sarah, Abraham, and his wife Hannah. It is also important to note that he freed his slave, Quaco, completely and gave him the equivalent of ten Spanish milled dollars. He also canceled the note Quaco owed to him of twenty Spanish dollars. (It is a lamentable fact that slave trading was common and legal during Colonial times. It is also true that Jacob Rodriguez Rivera, like many others, engaged in this practice. History is often difficult to excuse, but we can be glad that he did make this small symbolic gesture.)

Jacob Rodriguez Rivera was buried, like his cousin Aaron before him, at Newport Jewish Cemetery, where his remains are still honored today.

Dr. John de Sequeyra

*A Pioneer in the
Treatment of the Insane*

Dr. John de Sequeyra. De Sequeyra was educated at Leiden University, and appointed doctor in charge of the first public hospital in America, at Williamsburg. He kept written notes on the diseases in Virginia, especially of women.

WILLIAMSBURG became the second capital of the Colony of Virginia in 1699, after Jamestown, Virginia's first capital and America's first English settlement, had proved ill-suited to defense, to trade, and to agriculture. At that time, Williamsburg, a part of what was then called Middle Plantation, had only a few farmhouses and taverns. It did, however, have a college, the College of William and Mary, which still exists today, and the British Parish Church. These two institutions were the main reasons why Williamsburg was chosen for Virginia's new seat of government, along with an abundance of excellent farmland that would ensure economic success.

The new capital, according to the Colonial Williamsburg Foundation, was laid out along a mile-long axial street named for the Duke of Gloucester. At one end of the street was the Capitol and at the other end the Governor's Palace. The open spaces along the main street began filling up with houses, stores, and taverns.

Williamsburg soon became a complex urban community, with a pattern of work, family life, and cultural activities; it also became a marketplace for the surrounding communities, providing goods, services, religious activities, and general entertainment and diversion. Within Williamsburg's year-round population of two thousand souls, half of whom were slaves, there was a rich weaving of personal, familial, social, racial, and cultural relationships. It was an active and productive community.

This, then, was the city as Doctor John de Sequeyra first saw it when he arrived in 1745. Dr. de Sequeyra had been born in England in 1712 to Jewish parents of Spanish-Portuguese descent. He came from a line of ten generations of physicians, and he had taken his own medical degree in Leiden University in Holland in 1739, where he had studied with the famous Hermann Boerhaave, one of the world's leading enlightened medical scientists. The young student dedicated his graduating thesis to his brother, Dr. Joseph de Sequeyra, head doctor for the Portuguese in East India and Chief Physician of the Vice Regent of the Portuguese colony of Goa.

We do not know why Dr. John de Sequeyra chose to come to Williamsburg. We can speculate that his spirit of adventure prompted him to begin life in a new land. As soon as he arrived, he had to make a copy of his medical diploma, because the original had been confiscated when the ship that carried him to Virginia was captured by a French vessel. He then began to practice medicine in a multifaceted career that would last almost fifty years, during which time his many contributions to his own community and to the field of medical study would be numerous.

As soon as he began practicing medicine in Williamsburg, Dr. de Sequeyra began to keep a journal recording the diseases he encountered that were common to the colony of Virginia at that time. According to Harold B. Gill, historian, he kept this journal until 1781. In these records, he described the symptoms, such as bleeding, coughing, and vomiting, that accompanied the typical illnesses of the period. Some of the diseases he described are familiar to most people today, such as mumps, measles, chicken pox, whooping cough, and scarlet fever. Other records are of greater historical interest because they show what specific ailments bothered Virginians during the last half of the eighteenth century. These ailments included a variety of diseases encountered by children and ailing women. He also described in detail the treatments that patients suffering from these ailments had to endure.

For example, the intermittent fever that troubled Virginians in the year 1746 was probably due to malaria, and the "slow fever of Fibris Dysenteria," as Dr. de Sequeyra called it, may have been typhoid. The "putrid sore throat and rotten quinsy" was most probably caused by an outbreak of diphtheria. He mentions that smallpox was a constant threat.

"This fall produced intermittent fevers," he wrote in 1747.

There were scarlatine eruptions all over the body, a sickness of the stomach with vomiting and sometimes diarrhea. These were often purged...gently with salts, rhubarb and in the case of convulsed illness, vitriolated musk or castor oil was initiated. Sometimes, plentiful bleeding was necessary, with vitrious medicines given afterwards consisting of the compound powder of crab claws. This scarlatine fever has killed a great number of children.

In 1749, Dr. de Sequeyra wrote:

> The winter produced very violent colds, and these were epidemic all over the country. It was attended with a troublesome cough, pain on the head, hoarseness and fever. It was removed with plentiful of bleeding and spermaceti, made from whale oil, the drinking of hyssop tea or any other pectoral diluting drink.
>
> Pleurisies and pneumonias were becoming epidemic. Bleeding was often repeated and afterwards the patient was given rattlesnake root. In some part of the country, particularly along the borders of our rivers, many people died of these inflammations. Some felt a violent pain in the breast or the eye. I was informed that some died in 30 or 40 hours after they had been taken with it.

In 1752, Dr. de Sequeyra wrote of pleurisies accompanied by violent head pain or pain in the stomach toward the left arch of the diaphragm, with shortness of breath, low spirits, and, when the sufferer was near the end, black stools. The mortality rate was especially high among Negroes and pregnant women in these cases. "A private man from Gloucester, Virginia," wrote Dr. de Sequeyra, "acquainted me that he saved many people by giving a Vomit of Tartar Emetic." Another medicine often used was made from the herb coltsfoot with skimmed milk.

In addition to these year-by-year descriptions of various illnesses and diseases affecting his local area, Dr. de Sequeyra also wrote of the ailments of this new American country generally. He divided them into those of winter (including spring) and those of summer (including fall), the former being primarily of the inflammatory kind requiring bleeding and spermaceti, a form of whale oil. He also described slow nervous fevers of long durations and children's fevers chiefly caused by worms. There were malignant fevers of the bilious or putrid kind with violent pains in some parts of the body, causing a high fever and a quick pulse. And finally, Dr. de Sequeyra reported outbreaks of dysentery reaching epidemic proportions.

It was during this period of intense record-keeping that Dr. de Sequeyra often spoke with two of his close personal friends, William Pasteur and John

Instruments used by Dr. John de Sequeyra to "bleed" patients and cure them of hysteria and depression.

Galt, who were also prominent local physicians, and the doctors often conferred together about how to treat patients. In 1767, for example, the Virginia House of Burgesses, the reigning legal body in Virginia at the time, ordered "Dr. de Sequeyra, a physician, and Mr. Pasteur, a surgeon, to go to the County of York, and enquire into the state of health of James Pride who had refused to attend the House because of sickness." Three years later, Dr. de Sequeyra and Dr. Pasteur treated the English Governor of Williamsburg in his final fatal illness, "a bilious fever and St. Anthony's fire," for which the doctors prescribed bleeding the ailing ruler no fewer than seven times, easily extracting at least half the blood necessary for most normal bodies.

Among Dr. de Sequeyra's other patients were many of the most important citizens of the Williamsburg and surrounding areas, such as Carter Burwell of Carter's Grove Plantation and General George Washington's stepchildren, Martha and John Parke Custis. Dr. de Sequeyra was also known to Thomas Jefferson, who often visited the capital of Virginia to pursue his study of law and to visit George Wythe. In Jefferson's personal records, he credits one Dr.

de Sequeyra with the introduction of a new fruit into Virginia's culture, the tomato, which Dr. de Sequeyra proved was not poisonous.

In the 1760s and '70s, the houses and taverns of Williamsburg hosted many important political figures in the new movement toward the colonies' independence. More people involved with this movement could be walking along Williamsburg's streets at that time than in Philadelphia, Boston, or New York. Patrick Henry, William Bird II, and the Lees of Stratford, Virginia were just some of the notables there then, along with John Adams and George Washington. All of these men had one important link that tied them together both politically and emotionally. They had all fought against the British Crown for the removal of the Stamp Act.

From the British perspective, the resolution of that crisis was a serious blow, especially since it caused a loss of respect by the colonists for the Mother Country and the Crown in particular. In an effort to win back that respect from the colonists, Governor Fauquier, the Crown's representative in Williamsburg in 1767, was ordered to do a noble deed for the colonial citizens there. As a generous gesture, and to show that the Crown had the colonies' best interest at heart, the governor recommended the building of America's first public hospital exclusively for mental patients. In so doing, the Governor had to endorse legal confinement for those who could not help themselves.

The colonial legislators were not very impressed by this offer. They feared that the treatment of the insane was a real problem, alluding in their arguments to the most famous mental institution of the time, London's Bethlehem Hospital, whose nickname, "Bedlam," had become synonymous with "clamorous madness." It took two weeks for the colonial legislators to agree to the building of a "madhouse" in their midst.

But they did agree, and in 1771, work began on the project. The hospital's design was drawn by Robert Smith of Philadelphia, who had raised and built Carpenter Hall there and the Nassau House for a young college in New Jersey now known as Princeton. In Williamsburg, he designed an imposing brick building with a cypress shingled roof and one-and-a-half-inch flooring. The hospital needed to be secure to house "mad" people. It contained twenty-four cells or rooms and an apartment for the keeper and a meeting room for the supervising court of directors, which included George Wythe, as well as Peyton Randolph and John Randolph.

These men served without charge, reflecting Virginia's tradition of responsible leadership. They set the standards for the public hospital, and they had the final word on who would be admitted and who would be released. One of their first rules was to accept only those patients considered either

The Public Hospital in Williamsburg, Virginia, a gift of King George III to the colony. Here Dr. de Sequeyra attempted to cure mental patients who, for the first time in America, were removed from prisons for treatment.

dangerous or curable. They would not admit the classically harmless patients, alcoholics, paupers, or the like. This was not going to be either a prison or an extended care facility.

Get them in, get them cured, and get them out. That was the goal.

Dr. de Sequeyra was chosen as the first visiting physician of this public facility. His responsibility was to examine the patients upon their admission and also once a week thereafter. Since the number of patients rarely exceeded fifteen, with eight being the norm, Dr. de Sequeyra was easily able to perform this task while still continuing to pursue his practice of medicine.

Until the hospital opened, people of unsound mind had been imprisoned for lack of an alternative, to prevent mischief that could otherwise be done to or by them. Generally, insanity was divided into two rather broad categories:

Restored patient room, Public Hospital, Williamsburg. Some patients were restored to health and released from the facility to their own families.

the first was mania, a condition characterized by violent, restless, and frenzied behavior; and the second was melancholia, a disposition in which the person tended to be depressed, listless, and grief-stricken. At this time, the humours, or bodily fluids, were still being blamed for almost any human irregularity; but it was also commonly assumed that the mental patient willfully chose to be irrational and that insanity was caused by self-imposed lesions or ulcers to the brain, which caused one internal imbalance or another.

This being the thinking of the time, the mental patients under Dr. de Sequeyra's attention were often given strong physiological remedies. Primary among the therapeutic techniques practiced at the public hospital during its early years were powerful drugs, water treatments, bleeding instruments, blistering salves, and a whole group of restraining devices. Drugs were given to exhaust patients, stimulate them, sedate them, constrict their muscles, and induce constipation. Sometimes drugs would be used to cause diarrhea and vomiting. In addition, doctors often used water—sometimes hot, sometimes cold. In Williamsburg, the plunge booth or ducking chair was employed to exhaust or intimidate patients, while listless patients were dunked to elicit a lively response. Dr. de Sequeyra often blistered and bled patients, but according to some of his staff members, he also tried to use these remedies as moderately as possible for the patient's good. Dr. de Sequeyra believed that these procedures drained the system of harmful fluids, reduced inflammation, and refocused the patient's attention. When none of these treatments worked, and when a violent patient could not be restrained, often manacles or irons were put on by the local blacksmith. In such cases, the object was to induce the patient to reconsider his behavior and his mistaken choice of life as a lunatic.

Throughout all his years, Dr. de Sequeyra corresponded with other learned men of his time, always willing to try any state-of-the-art procedure possible to help his patients. Because of this interest, he eventually learned to diagnose his patients by phrenology, learning from the bumps on their heads, locating them, and then administering jolts of static electricity from an electric generator, the latest technique.

Dr. de Sequeyra's success rates in restoring reason "to the mad" are recorded in Williamsburg papers of the time. During the hospital's first five years, thirty-eight patients were treated, of whom eighteen were restored to sanity and discharged, seven were deemed well enough to go to the care of family and friends, three died, and ten were left in confinement. Whether or not these results were acceptable to the governing supervisors, or to the community for that matter, we do not know.

The Revolutionary War closed the hospital, since funds from the British monarchy were no longer available. The hospital remained closed until 1787, when it reopened as a Virginia state-supported facility.

The post that Dr. de Sequeyra assumed at Williamsburg involved two important new concepts. The first was that "mad" people should not be housed with prisoners. They should be separated. This was about as enlightened as those times got. The second principle was that a public hospital did not exist simply to keep and house these people. Dr. de Sequeyra actually tried to cure them and return them to society. His role, and the hospital's, was active, not passive. In this he was truly ahead of his time.

We still have the letters that Dr. de Sequeyra wrote to the governors of Virginia giving them the required hospital reports. These reports, along with his volume describing the diseases of Virginia, are housed today at the S.W.E.M. Library at the College of William and Mary, a part of the Galt Collection. They can be seen in Williamsburg today, as can a re-creation erected in 1985 of America's first public hospital. Visitors to Williamsburg can also visit Shield's Tavern, where Dr. de Sequeyra resided for the last twenty-one years of his life.

At the time of his death at age eighty-two, Dr. de Sequeyra had served as a doctor in Williamsburg for fifty years. An obituary in a South Carolina newspaper called him "an eminent physician who worked in a new field, a public hospital for the insane." A Richmond newspaper described him as "a most important and famous physician."

The Gratz Family

Early Pioneers of
Westward Expansion

Michael Gratz. A successful merchant in Phila-
delphia, Gratz supported Congregation Mikveh
Israel and Benjamin Franklin's Free Library.
He saw to it that the Jewish community signed
the non-importation agreement, which
said to England that there would be
no taxation without representation.

IN THE history of early Philadelphia, Gratz is a very important name. The two brothers, Barnard and Michael, contributed enormously, not only to the Jewish community there but to the general community of the city; and in time the Gratz family became an important part of American history because of their role in the movement that was to become known as Westward Expansion.

When Barnard Gratz arrived in Philadelphia in 1754, there was already an established Jewish community there. It is believed that Jews traveled that way along the Delaware River to trade with the Indian tribes, some as early as 1690. By the 1730s, Philadelphia had become a growing center of trade with England and other European cities.

In 1737, Nathan Levy helped establish a solid Jewish community in Philadelphia. Nathan had been born in 1704, the son of Moses Levy, a well-known New York merchant and president of the Spanish-Portuguese congregation, Shearith Israel. Nathan became a part of the Philadelphia colonial trade as both a merchant and a ship owner. He was joined in business by his nephew, David Franks, the son of another New York merchant, Jacob Franks. Since both the Franks and the Levy families had come to America from London, the new partnership had solid international business connections. Ships from the Levy Franks company carried various types of cargo. In fact, in 1752, one of

Nathan Franks's ships, the *Myrtilla*, carried a bell that had been ordered by the Pennsylvania colony for its new state house. That bell would one day be known as the Liberty Bell.

Barnard Gratz was born in upper Silesia, Poland. He lived in London for five years, working for a cousin and learning the English language; he also learned as much as he could about the art of business. In 1754, he arrived in Philadelphia and went to work for David Franks's mercantile and trading organization. After seven years, he went into business for himself. Following in his older brother's footsteps Michael Gratz

The Liberty Bell, brought to America on the ship Myrtilla, *owned by David Franks and Nathan Levy of Philadelphia. The bell was originally ordered for use at the Pennsylvania statehouse, before it became a symbol of America's freedom from England.*

came to Philadelphia in 1759, and also worked for David Franks, where he learned the ways of the American colonial merchant.

The two brothers were not alike. Barnard was considered a serious and responsible person, whereas Michael was thought of as a dandy, because he bought himself fancy breeches and silver buckles, even when he couldn't afford such finery. His love of beautiful material objects made Michael want to succeed, and in fact he bought and surrounded himself with magnificent objects throughout his lifetime.

Their personal habits aside, the brothers were well matched, and soon after Michael's arrival in Philadelphia they joined in a partnership called B&M Gratz. This business relationship was to have an important effect on Philadelphia and the rest of the colonies.

In 1760, on one of his business trips to New York, Barnard married Richa Cohen, the daughter of Samuel Myers Cohen. This was an important union, because it connected Barnard with a number of other important Jewish businessmen. Richa's brother married the daughter of Joseph Simon, a pillar of the Lancaster, Pennsylvania Jewish business community; and one of her sisters married Mathias Bush, another successful Pennsylvania merchant; while yet another sister, Elkalah, married the famous New York silversmith, Myer Myers.

It was through Barnard's business network that Michael also became acquainted with Joseph Simon of Lancaster, Pennsylvania. He married another of Joseph's daughters, Miriam. The business ties between New York and Pennsylvania were strengthened because of these two marriages, which facilitated trading of goods and new opportunities becoming available at every turn. Some of the wares they traded included rice, tobacco, corn, cordials, bourbon whisky, brandy, foodstuffs, tools, and various luxuries such as cloth, sugar, molasses, coffee, and spices.

In 1765 Michael Gratz made a trip to the the West Indies. He returned to Philadelphia with an innovative idea, that of exporting kosher meat. The West Indian Islands depended on imports for their food, and Michael saw the economic advantages of sending them their meat and fat.

To meet the ritual requirements, the meat could not be sent fresh, because the trip took longer than the three days allowed by Jewish law for fresh meat. Therefore, the meat was carefully slaughtered according to law, boiled and salted and properly packed in large kegs, making it possible for the food to reach the islands without the danger of contamination—either bacterial or ritual. This operation had to be approved by the Jewish law and a certificate had to be issued called a "Hekscher." The nearest religious authority was in New York. There Abraham Abrahams, the local New York Shochet, after surveying the Gratz plan, declared that the Jews of Barbados could eat the contents of the barrels sent by the Gratz brothers. This is believed to be the earliest Hekscher granted in America. This same certificate allowed the Gratz brothers to export meat to other places as well. The kosher meat export company was a brilliant idea, and just one example of the the forward thinking, ingenuity, and keen business sense that made Barnard and Michael Gratz excellent merchants.

The Gratz brothers were also a vital part of the adventure in opening up the western part of Pennsylvania. They helped to make agreements in 1776 with the Shawnee and Delaware at Fort Pitt, making it safe for themselves and other traders to work. Barnard and Michael went to the frontier, often on horseback, for days at a time to trade with the Indians for furs and pelts. Their full confidence in the potential of the new market and their willingness to invest in it set an important example for other merchants who joined the nation's western expansion.

Hekscher, *or certificate to ensure that meat is kosher, granted to Michael and Bernard Gratz, who export-ed meat to the Caribbean. This is believed to be the first* hekscher *granted in America.*

On one such trip to the frontier, Michael wrote a letter home to his brother in Philadelphia. The letter, which was written in Yiddish, closes as follows: "I have to stop now, Barnard, soon it will be the beginning of Shabbos."

Back in Philadelphia, both Michael and Barnard took a role in political causes against the British monarchy. Both brothers signed the Non-Importation Resolution that protested taxation without representation. When the English Parliament imposed heavy taxes on goods imported into the American colonies in 1765, the citizens of the colonies joined together in an effort to force the king to withdraw the levied fines. Non-importation agreements were written in each of the major cities of the colonies, including New York and Philadelphia. Among the people supporting the Non-Importation Resolution were Jewish merchants, many of whom were directly affected by Great Britain's actions. When the Revolutionary War was declared, the Gratz brothers helped to manufacture and supply gun powder and fire arms to Washington's troops. When Jews from other colonies came to Philadelphia for safe haven during the war, the Gratz brothers saw to it that they were made a welcome part of the Philadelphia community.

* * *

Active in the Congregation Mikveh Israel, the Gratz brothers were also contributors to the new public library in Philadelphia, known as the Free Library, which was started by Benjamin Franklin. Eighteenth-century Philadelphia was a major center for style, and much of the furniture that was made there was based on syles found in the fashionable Thomas Chippendale pattern book that could have been in the Free Library. We can only imagine that Michael Gratz was pleased about the connection, because of his own purchases of beautiful furniture. (Many of his personal furnishings, including his desk and bookcase, were later purchased by Henry DuPont and are now housed at Winterthur, DuPont's home in Delaware.) Michael and Miriam needed a lot of furniture, for they had twelve children, all healthy and growing.

In both brothers' households, there were large libraries filled with many books. One of Michael's daughters, Rebecca, was active in literary circles, and she numbered among her friends such literary figures as Washington Irving and Sir Walter Scott. She was supposedly the model for the Jewish heroine of the most popular novel of the day, Sir Walter Scott's *Ivanhoe*, though Rebecca never identified herself as the heroine.

Rebecca was, however, a heroine in her own right. Along with her mother and her sisters, she distinguished herself as an original member of the Female Association for the Relief of Women and Children in Reduced Circumstances when it was founded in 1801. Toward this community undertaking she devoted an energy that typified her entire life. She offered herself as a teacher of the Hebrew language and grammar to the children of Philadelphia's Jewish community. In 1814 she helped organize the Orphans' Society, a nonsectarian charity whose seat was the Presbyterian Church.

Like her father, Rebecca collected beautiful objects as a patroness of the arts. She had her portrait painted by Thomas Sully, the famous eighteenth-century portraitist. But Rebecca was only one of the successful Gratz offspring. Her cousin, Rachel Gratz, married Benjamin Etting in 1790 and moved to Baltimore, Maryland, where they helped establish the Jewish community. They, too, had their portraits painted by Thomas Sully. They collected hundreds of pieces of furniture, porcelain, and paintings; most of their belongings can now be seen in the Maryland Historical Society in Baltimore.

Simon Gratz, Rebecca's brother, helped start the Gratz Liberal College for the Arts and Sciences in Philadelphia. He also sat on the board of the Pennsylvania Academy of Fine Arts. Both of these important institutions are still viable forces in Philadelphia today. His brother, Benjamin, helped found Gratzville, Kentucky, which remains as Gratz Park, a residential neighborhood. The Gratzville Park community center still exists in Lexington today.

The Philadelphia mahogany chest belonging to Michael Gratz. The extensive carving, shell design, and flame finials are in keeping with the highest style of the period.

The Philadelphia mahogany side chair, circa 1770, made for Michael Gratz. With an open splat in the back and ball-and-claw feet, it is in the Chippendale style. This and other pieces in Gratz's collection are today housed at the Winterthur Museum in Delaware.

Jacob Gratz, another of Rebecca's brothers, was both a Pennsylvania state representative and then a state senator in 1807.

The list of accomplishments by this remarkable family goes on and on. Their contributions to Philadelphia, Baltimore, and eventually the state of Kentucky were generous and far reaching, and they form an important part of the fabric of early American Jewish history.

Rebecca Gratz, daughter of Michael and Miriam Gratz. A philanthropist, she was a Sunday school teacher and a contributor to the School for the Deaf and Dumb. With her mother she helped to form a society for the financial relief of women and children in reduced circumstances.

Joseph Simon

Entrepreneur, Frontiersman, and Patriot

JOSEPH Simon lived on the frontier lands of Lancaster, Pennsylvania. Originally from Poland, he became a naturalized citizen of Pennsylvania in 1749. He was married to Rosa Bunn, the niece of Samuel Myers Cohen of New York.

Simon was the leading merchant in Lancaster, as well as a successful land owner and Indian trader in the Pennsylvania Dutch country surrounding the town. In 1767 the Reverend Thomas Barton of Lancaster introduced Joseph Simon to William Johnson as "a worthy, honest Jew and principal merchant of this place, who has always been employed as a victullar to the troops who have been quartered here and has given general satisfaction." Eager to improve trade routes to and from Lancaster, Simon helped to establish and maintain the Lancaster Pike, which still exists today.

But Simon's business dealings and his vision went far beyond Lancaster, for he was one of the main proponents of westward expansion in early America. His ventures took him into western Pennsylvania and out into Kentucky and Ohio, which were then still a part of the Virginia Commonwealth. He also acquired land in Illinois, and he helped finance one of the first Illinois expeditions, made by George Croghan in 1765, providing that expedition with two thousand pounds' worth of goods to be traded with the Indians, including clothing, blankets, hair trinkets, silver arm bands, ear bells, and hair plates.

Trading for furs was the main business occupation of Joseph Simon's life, but owning stakes in parcels of land was his most successful venture. His interests in the Grand Ohio Scheme called "The Indiana" and his plan to settle communities near Louisville, Kentucky occupied most of his legal activities. Always interested in trading in these new western areas, he strived to have clear titles to lands there. Having land in Illinois, Simon was one of nine men who

Lintel of Torah ark in the home of Joseph Simon in Lancaster, Pennsylvania. There was no synagogue in Lancaster, so religious services were held at Simon's home.

asked for the original Indian deed on his land grant so that it could be recorded in Virginia.

Joseph Simon also played an important part in the Revolutionary War, showing his loyalty by supplying the soldiers of the Continental Congress with blankets for their military hospital, rifles and drums for the army, and provisions for prisoners, women, and children. He also promised in 1777 to help provide people to serve as information carriers between Lancaster and General Washington's army.

Throughout his life and his business career, Joseph Simon maintained close connections with other influential Jewish entrepreneurs. He had many business transactions with Nathan Levy and David Franks, both merchants from Philadelphia. Their wagons would travel to Lancaster to bring much-needed goods like tools for building houses and working the land and cloth to make wearing apparel. Their trade also went from Lancaster to Fort Duquesne, later to be called Pittsburgh.

Joseph Simon also had business dealings with Michael and Barnard Gratz, important merchants and political figures in Philadelphia. Eventually Michael Gratz married Joseph Simon's daughter, Miriam. Michael and Miriam had twelve children, of whom Rebecca was the best known for her work in social reform. She helped to found the first Hebrew Sunday school in America.

Another of Joseph Simon's daughters, Shinah, married a man named Nicholas Schuyler, who was a member of New York society but was not Jewish. This "out of Judaism union" upset Joseph Simon terribly, and he never really accepted Shinah back into his life again until he was on his deathbed,

Page from the will of Joseph Simon of Lancaster. Active in trade with the Indian tribes west of Lancaster, Simon provided everything from scarlet cloth and blankets to looking glasses and bells.

Joseph Simon ———————————————————————— 85

when he sent for her, forgave her, blessed her, and then died in her arms.

It is apparent from this family episode that Joseph Simon adhered faithfully to his Jewish religion. He had a small synagogue in his home in Lancaster; the lintel from the ark in that synagogue is now at the American Jewish Historical Society. Simon also employed his own shochet to kill and prepare all of his meat, so that he could keep to the rules of Kashrut, or being kosher.

Joseph Simon was one of the first trustees of Congregation Mikveh Israel to preside over the burial grounds for the use of the whole Jewish community in Philadelphia. He was also instrumental in borrowing a Torah scroll from Congregation Shearith Israel in New York before Mikveh Israel had either a scroll or a building of its own.

When Simon died in 1804, he left a will that specifically named only two heirs, his daughters, Bilah Simon Cohen and Leah Simon Phillips. Both received 7,500 acres of land in southeastern Pennsylvania. The will also left his family silverplate, which was used for religious worship, and two rolls containing the five books of Moses, the Torah, to the congregation Mikveh Israel, but only after the death of one of his sons-in-law, Levy Phillips, who was to have the use of them during his lifetime.

As an entrepreneur, frontiersman, and patriot, as well as a pillar in his Jewish community, Joseph Simon's efforts have been respected and his contributions have long been remembered.

Abigail Minis

*An Early
American Innkeeper*

Sterling silver chalice belonging to Philip Minis, in the flared, Rococo style of the mid-eighteenth century. Today it is housed at the Georgia Historical Society in Savannah.

ABIGAIL Minis and her husband, Abraham, were among the original members of the Jewish community of Savannah, Georgia. They came to the new colony from England in 1733, only a few months after it was founded by Governor James Oglethorpe. Originally a buffer zone to protect wealthy South Carolina from the threat of being overrun by the Spaniards, who already occupied Florida, Georgia was the last of the original thirteen colonies to be settled. Savannah, then, was a frontier town that divided the known civilization from the uncharted and unknown regions beyond.

The year 1733 was also when Governor Oglethorpe granted the first parcels of land to anyone inhabiting Georgia, including Abraham and Abigail Minis. By 1736, Abraham Minis had accumulated four acres of a garden lot and ten acres of a farm from which he cultivated thirty-six bushels of Indian corn. It was at this point that Abigail and Abraham also became ranchers, raising cattle on a large scale, and starting in 1740 they called their ranch the "A&M," and they developed an appropriate A&M brand. By this time they were raising crops not only for their own use, but also for sale or trade to others.

Abraham and Abigail were entrepreneurs who, through their acquisitions and other businesses, became very successful. Branching out, they organized a prosperous merchandising business, using both their own home-grown products and goods they imported from England. Abraham was even known to use his small boat to deliver provisions for Governor Oglethorpe during his numerous expeditions and raids against the Spaniards.

In 1757, quite suddenly, Abraham Minis died, leaving Abigail, at age fifty-six a working mother now with nine children. It must have taken much perseverance, drive, and guts to carry on, but that's what she did. She completely took over the operation of the ranches, farms, a store, and even a family-run tavern which she operated out of their home.

To accomplish all of this work, Abigail needed help, and for that purpose she owned between fifteen and twenty slaves. According to all records, she treated these slaves humanely, providing them with an abundance of shelter and food and other human necessities.

As a widow, Abigail began to expand her horizons even farther. She obtained another 2,329 acres to farm or ranch, in addition to two town lots in Savannah. Her eagerness to acquire more property for the support of her large family became her passion. Learning the art of getting along in a tough frontier environment, she developed a shrewd business acumen, which may account for the fact that an early survey of one of her Savannah properties showed only thirty-seven taxable acres, whereas a later survey proved that it contained seventy-four acres.

Perhaps because Abigail was both a mother and a business woman she developed a special talent for hospitality. She provided a full table and an open door to her family, friends, neighbors, and paid guests. Beginning in 1756, a year before Abraham's death, the Minis home was also a shop and a tavern on one of Savannah's main streets. The dwelling included five rooms, a garret or attic, and a kitchen. One of the five rooms in the house was the counting house, where all of the accounts were kept for all of the many Minis's business transactions. Because it was also a tavern, beds were placed all over the house. In the eighteenth century, a tavern guest usually rented a bed or a part of a bed rather than an entire room. Abigail referred to one of the rooms as the "new room," which suggests that the house may have been added onto for this purpose. Every room, according to the Minis inventory book of 1757, was cluttered with beds for her customers—even the garret, the kitchen, and the counting house.

> The new room contained two tables, a bed, a bedstead with white curtains, two pillows, a blanket and quilt, a clothespress and looking glass, and a pair of iron dogs for the fireplace. The middle room had a looking glass, two tables, and a pair of fire dogs. In a small area joining the middle room was a bed with bolster, pillow, blanket, quilt, and table. The garret held a desk, a couch, two small beds, and a box

bedstead. Mrs. Minis set up additional beds in both her shop and counting house. The shop too had a bed with bolster, blanket, quilt, two pillows, a small looking glass, and a table. This room was probably long, as there were thirteen chairs in the room.

In colonial times, chairs would have been placed along walls until they were needed for entertaining. Thirteen chairs lined up along a wall would have needed a lot of linear space.

As a homemaker, Abigail was known to be firm and precise in her manner. She also supervised all of the domestic chores required of a colonial homemaker, including the cooking done in the fireplace and training of the household servants. The inventory of the kitchen tells us much about colonial cooking in general, even though the Minis kitchen was probably better stocked than most other kitchens because it was often obliged to provide food for paying guests. There was a pair of firedogs to hold the logs in the fireplace, a tack (hanging shelf), an iron dripping pan for the grease, a frying pan, two iron skillets, two pothooks, three iron pots, two iron pans, two brass kettles, a tin fish kettle, two tea kettles, two coffeepots, a copper gallon pot, two brass lamps, a warming pan, and seven candlesticks. At the kitchen table, where presumably both family and guests ate, were two benches and four stools. There were six tablecloths. The kitchen could be set up with three cots also and transformed into a bedroom.

From that kitchen, on King George III's birthday in 1772, Abigail served a company of seventy distinguished celebrants. Moreover, the Minis tavern was often called upon to be the eighteenth-century take-out establishment, providing packaged food and liquor for guests and passersby to purchase for their next day's journey.

The War for Independence interrupted Abigail's life and her business. At this point she was a successful independent entrepreneur. At a time when the typical Jewish colonial woman was expected to tend only to her kosher kitchen, Abigail was supplying General Washington's revolutionary troops with agricultural products from her farms and ranch, including large supplies of grain and meat provisions—and all of that with only a promise of eventual payment for her services.

Having supplied these goods to the colonial forces, however, she was branded an enemy of the British, so she decided it was better not to remain in her home town as long as Savannah was occupied and controlled by British troops. In October 1779, she petitioned the British General Wright and the royal court for permission to leave with her children for the safer ground of Charleston, South Carolina. Because of her many business dealings, she had developed many friendships with important people, including some of the British elite. General Wright was one such friend, and he helped her secure safe passage out of Savannah. By then a seventy-year-old matriarch, Abigail took her five daughters with her and settled down in Charleston, while her sons stayed in Georgia, where they contributed to the Revolutionary War effort.

Abigail wrote the following letter from Charleston during the Revolutionary War to her friend Mordecai Sheftall, a fellow Savannahan, then residing in Philadelphia. In the letter, she asked Sheftall for his help in obtaining payment for the goods she had delivered to the revolutionary forces.

> Mordacai Sheftall, Esqr.
> Philadelphia
> Charleston Jan'y 14
> Dear Sir,
>
> Inclosed I have sent you a copy of certificates given me for sundry Articles provision, &c, &c delivered the Allied Army when before the lines of Savannah in September 1779 immediately after the Surrender of this Town to the British I gave the Original Certificated to General Lincoln who promised to have settled and paid, but the communication between Philadelphia and this place being totally stopt [I] have not heard from him.
>
> I have since made application to Col. Wylly the then Acting Quarter Master General for a settlement of the same, he informs me he cannot do anything in the matter unless the original certificates were here.
>
> I have to request that you will make particular Enquiry of General Lincoln or any officer who may have the papers belonging to this department in their possession for them, and use every method to obtain the money, in case you should obtain it I must request you to lay it out or do with it as will turn out best for my Interest—in case nothing can be done to the Northward with them please find or keep them until I can receive them without risque.
>
> Myself and daughters present our Compliments.
> I am your obed. Serv.
> Abigail Minis

These were difficult times for many people, but this letter demonstrates Abigail's clear head for business and her ability to communicate concisely, politely, and firmly.

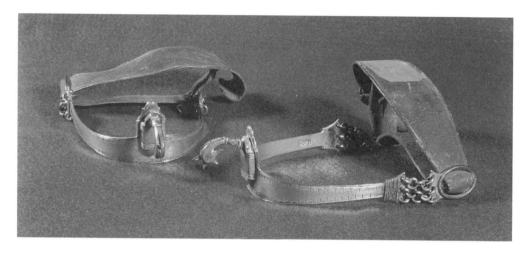

Sterling silver spurs used by Philip Minis, the first white male born in Georgia. Philip's parents, Abraham and Abigail, came to Savannah in 1733, shortly after Governor George Oglethorpe arrived. Philip used these spurs when he rode out to the frontier to trade goods with the Indians. He was a founder of the Mickve Israel Congregation in Savannah, serving as its Parness or President, and took part in the Revolutionary War.

Abigail Minis was also a strict mother. She had to be, for she kept her family very close, making sure their children all received a fine education, including learning the ways of being both observant Jews and loyal and respected colonial citizens. Her heirs proved that she was successful.

Her son, Philip, was dedicated to the revolutionary cause. At one time, he even provided a total of $10,918.50 to cover the salaries of the North Carolina regiment and the Virginia regiment and provisions for all the Continental troops in South Carolina. In 1776 Philip served as acting paymaster and a commissioner of the Georgia regimental forces. At the end of the Revolutionary War, he was hailed as a hero by General Washington.

In his civil life, Philip was named by Mordecai Sheftall to be an original trustee of the first Jewish burial grounds in Savannah, and in July 1786 Philip became the Parnass or President of the Portuguese-Spanish Synagogue in Savannah, Mickve Israel. He took his responsibilities for his Jewish community very seriously, having had a good teacher in his mother. Mickve Israel Synagogue is still in existence in Savannah today.

One of Philip's brothers, Isaac Minis, served as the fire chief of the city of Savannah in 1809, and in 1815 he was chosen as the Chatham County representative to the Georgia State Legislature.

The Minis family still exists in Savannah today. They are still strong supporters of their Mickve Israel congregation and take much pride in the Jewish

Judith Pollack Minis, wife of Philip Minis. Judith was born in Newport, Rhode Island, and although she resided in Savannah, she was buried in the Newport cemetery.

community, even though for many years now most of the family are practicing Christians. Today in Savannah there exists Minis Avenue, named for Abigail and her family.

The history of Abigail Minis is important because she knew that a woman had the right to pursue her own goals as well as her own career. While her husband was alive, she was a close partner in the family economy, and after he died, she took up his role completely. For some families even today, the death of a husband and father spells catastrophe. Often the wife can do nothing more than witness the erosion of familial control. Abigail managed to retain not only that control, but a high level of grace and humanity as well.

In assuming all of these responsibilities, Abigail showed an ease and a readiness to embrace and accept her circumstances. In doing so, she exhibited talent, patriotism, and business prowess, overcoming prejudice in a world normally dominated by men, thereby leaving a small door open for generations to follow.

Abigail died in 1794 at the age of ninety-three. In her will, Abigail honored and thanked her five daughters: "I give and devise and bequeath all of my estate, real and personal and of what nature soever, and wherever to be found to my five Daughters, Leah Minis, Esther Minis, Judith Minis, Hannah Minis, and Sarah Minis, who with great affection, have always treated me as their fond Mother, and by their Industry have helped not only to gain what I Possess, but by their frugality to keep together my Estate." None of her five daughters married until after Abigail's death.

When one thinks of the typical colonial American woman, Abigail Minis stands out as remarkable. But in any society, Abigail would be recognized as a woman of innumerable talents and accomplishments. She did what she had to do to survive and prosper as a single woman in eighteenth-century America.

The Sheftalls of Savannah

Heroes of the Revolution

Miniature portrait of Mordecai Sheftall, meant to be worn on a ribbon or chain around the neck. Notice his waistcoat and vest, and that his hair is in a ponytail. Sheftall was one of the founders of the Jewish community in Savannah, Georgia, where he helped to establish Mickve Israel Synagogue and donated land for a Jewish cemetery. He also supported the Orphans' Society, as did his father before him.

SAVANNAH, Georgia, was the only colony to have an organized Jewish immigration. Founded in 1733 by Governor James Oglethorpe, Georgia was formed to protect South Carolina from invasion by the Spanish, who then occupied the area now called Florida. Under the circumstances, it was difficult to persuade people to come to Georgia; the English had to offer passage to people to go there, and the people who accepted that offer included beggars and prisoners. Then, in July 1733, the Portuguese-Spanish community of London decided to send a group of Jews who had been coming into their community from Poland and Germany. That brought ninety Jewish people to the new colony of Georgia.

Governor Oglethorpe, who had arrived just five months earlier, was not happy about having a large Jewish population to absorb into his colony. But one of the newcomers was a Dr. Samuel Nunes Ribeira, who helped stop a wide-spreading epidemic in Savannah. This act of unselfish public human kindness by Dr. Ribeira made it much easier for Governor Oglethorpe to welcome the Jews.

In spite of this welcome, Savannah was not an easy place for anyone to live. There were huge economic restrictions. For example, no one could own the land he worked; only the Trustees of the Colony in England had that right. Another problem for the newcomers to this agriculture-based economy was that Georgia at that time did not allow slavery. These two laws adversely affected the livelihoods of the farmers of Georgia, including the Jewish farmers, and many of them left the area. More settlers left Georgia in 1740 when the Spanish in Florida threatened to conquer Georgia; this included all of the Spanish-Portuguese Jewish community, who feared another Inquisition. That left only two Jewish families in Savannah at that time, the Minis family and the Sheftalls, both having Ashkenazic roots.

In 1759, the Trustees of Georgia agreed to allow private ownership of land and also decided to permit the importation of slaves. By this time the Spanish were no longer posing a threat, so many of the original settlers of Georgia who had fled now came back, including much of the Jewish population.

A second exile occurred during the Revolutionary War. Most of the Savannahan Jews were not loyal to the Crown, and so they left town before the British troops conquered the city on December 29, 1778. It was not until after the Revolution that Savannah's Jewish population returned to stay. The task before them was to rebuild the community back to the active level it had reached before the Revolution. This was accomplished primarily with the help of Mordecai Sheftall.

Mordecai Sheftall's father, Benjamin Sheftall, came to Savannah in 1733. He brought with him a Torah that is still owned by Mickve Israel today. Growing up in Savannah, in 1771 Mordecai married Frances Hart, from Charleston, South Carolina. Mordecai prospered, and by the time of the Revolution he

Frances Sheftall, wife of Mordecai Sheftall, in the typical dress of the day, with a white bib on her dark dress.

had achieved economic success as a merchant and as a large landowner. He was involved in timbering, shipping, and the retailing of manufactured goods. He was also a leader of the community. He was instrumental in organizing their synagogue, Mickve Israel, and he was responsible for arranging for a permanent Jewish burial ground in 1773, with land that had been granted to him by King George III.

During the Revolutionary War, Mordecai Sheftall contributed significantly to the war effort. When no funds were forthcoming from General Washington, the Sheftall family helped to provide money for food and provisions for the soldiers fighting in South Carolina and Georgia. Mordecai served in the army, as did his son, Sheftall Sheftall. Both were captured at the Battle of Savannah when the city fell to British troops in 1779 and were imprisoned temporarily on the island of Antigua and then spent the rest of the war in Philadelphia, helping to form the Synagogue Mikveh Israel. (Sheftall Sheftall, as a Revolutionary War veteran and hero, remained a prominent member of Savannah society. He continued to wear out-of-fashion colonial-style clothing,

Sign at the Jewish cemetery in Savannah, Georgia, established by Mordecai Sheftall on land granted to him by George III of England.

Nellie Bush Sheftall, wife of Moses Sheftall. Originally from Charleston, South Carolina, Nellie was considered a beauty. She is shown in the typical dress of her day, with a ruffle at the neck and her hair in a tight coif with a feathered hat.

including a three-cornered hat, which earned him the nickname "Cocked-Hat Sheftall.")

After the war, Mordecai played an active role in the Jewish community of Savannah, as well as in the general society of Georgia. He helped to establish religious schools and charitable organizations. He served in the state legislative body of Georgia for six years. He was a member of the Georgia Union Society, as was his father before him; this was an organization formed to further the education of orphaned children. He was also a Mason, a part of the Solomon Lodge, which still houses his Mason's apron today. He campaigned for human rights and constantly worked at bridging the gap between the Jewish and Gentile communities.

It is important to note that he accomplished all of this at the same time he was trying to rebuild his own life. A patriot in every sense of the word, he had used most of the fortune had had amassed before the Revolution to help the fight against the British. On November 21, 1780, he wrote to Samuel Huntington, the president of the United States Congress, asking for the pay he was owed for having served in the army and for having "sacrificed everything in the cause of his country." No funds were ever returned to Mordecai by the United States government.

Nevertheless, Mordecai Sheftall and his family prospered and were well respected in Georgia society. Mordecai's son Moses carried on the family tradition of public service. He studied medicine at the University of Pennsylvania under the famous Dr. Benjamin Rush, one of the signers of the Declaration of Independence. He became a doctor in 1790 was elected twice to the legislative body of Georgia, and later served as a country judge.

Today many descendants of the Sheftall family still reside in Savannah, and, as part of the Jewish community they are still giving financial support to their beloved Mickve Israel Congregation.

Haym Salomon

He Helped Finance
the American Revolution

AYM Salomon was born in Lissa, Poland, in 1740. In about 1775 he arrived in New York City and entered business as a merchant. In the ten years that remained of his life, he was to become one of America's most prominent Jewish citizens and one of the most important financial supporters of the American colonies during the Revolutionary War.

Haym Salomon. A financier, Salomon sold bonds to raise the funds that General Washington needed to fight the Revolutionary War.

In 1777 he married Rachel Franks, the daughter of Moses B. Franks, a merchant. He had an office at 22 Wall Street, which he advertised as a bank auction house that would accept all types of merchandise for sale.

New York City was occupied by the British during the Revolutionary War, and that caused a crisis for Haym. In August of 1778, he was accused by the British of being a spy for the American Rebels, and of being part of a plot to burn King George's fleet of ships and destroy the British warehouses in the New York area. He was arrested and condemned to death. Able to bribe those who guarded him with gold coins, he escaped the Provost Prison and the city of New York and fled to Philadelphia, where he began to reestablish himself in the business community there. He became a commission business broker and dealt in the sale of bills of exchange.

The rapid success of his Philadelphia enterprise brought him responsibilities in other areas of life as well, including responsibilities in the Jewish community of that city. He became part of the governing council of the synagogue, Mikveh Israel, and eventually he became its most generous contributor. He also assumed the job of treasurer of Philadelphia's Ezrath Orechim, the society of indigent travelers, one of America's first Jewish charitable

The second building of Synagogue Mikveh Israel, Philadelphia. Haym Salomon and the Gratz brothers were among the synagogue's many benefactors. Many artifacts from this building are housed in the present synagogue in Philadelphia.

organizations. Finally, he served on America's first Bet Din, the Rabbinic Court of Arbitration, which settled disputes of every kind concerning synagogue activities, ritual observances, marriages, and divorces. Throughout all of his businesses as well as in his civic responsibilities, Salomon was known as a scrupulously devout Jew. His newspaper advertisements stated that he did "no business on Saturdays, the Shabbat."

Haym Salomon and his family lived above and behind his business office on Front Street, between Arch and Market Streets, an active area for com-

Samuel Hays. Hays was a merchant engaged in trade with the Far East, and learned to broker bonds when he worked for Haym Salomon. Committed to the city of Philadelphia, he served as a member of the Philadelphia Chamber of Commerce and subscribed to the Chestnut Street Theater in 1793.

merce in Philadelphia. Although his living quarters were not spacious, he did enjoy some luxury with the purchase of new mahogany furniture and silverplate for his table. He had a modest image, however, and was not known to have acquired many expensive goods.

Salomon's business included, as he advertised, bills of exchange for all parts of Europe. He left behind bank notes representing loans to both Holland and France. His brilliance as a financial mediator, moving around dozens of currencies at a time, was noticed by Robert Morris, the Superintendent of the Office of Finance for the New Colonial Congress, who offered Haym the position of Broker to the Office of Finance. By accepting this offer, Haym became the sole broker in the sale of bills of exchange, borrowing the money that the Congress needed to to maintain the American government during the period from 1780 to 1785. In this job, Salomon became the principal individual depositor to the Bank of North America during the Revolutionary period.

Robert Morris's diary, starting with May 11, 1781, mentions the help of Haym Salomon no fewer than 114 times in seventy-five different financial transactions on behalf of Congress. He raised as much as eight hundred thousand dollars; he also contributed much of his own funds to aid the Congress and the American Revolutionary cause. Salomon was able to help the cause he believed in, at a time when the new country's revenues were at their lowest point and there was no one else to help.

Statue of George Washington congratulating Robert Morris and Haym Salomon for helping to raise money for the Revolutionary War.

Although Haym's contributions of expertise and funds were invaluable to the new nation, most people at the time were unaware of his services and therefore his generosity and his genius were unknown to the public during his lifetime. Only a few officials from the government were aware of his devotion to his adopted country, and only a few knew that Robert Morris's success in arranging the financing of the Revolution depended on the work of this unsung hero.

During this time Haym also had other interests. In 1784, he co-sponsored the construction of a hot air balloon; that project was never completed, but if the balloon had gotten off the ground it would have been the first balloon flight in America. The same year he took the time to respond to an article in the Philadelphia *Independent Gazeteer* concerning a statement delivered by a Miers Fisher in the Assembly of Pennsylvania which slandered the Jews.

Haym Salomon died on January 6, 1785, at the age of forty-five. By this time, the Revolutionary War was over, and Haym died poor and in debt, having loaned so much of his own money to Congress. He had planned to return to New York to reestablish himself as a financial broker, but he never had the chance to do that, and he was buried unceremoniously in the Mikveh Israel Cemetery in Philadelphia. His widow and their children were left without any means to raise the money they needed to live. Eventually Rachel remarried; her new husband, David Halbrun, was a person not of the Jewish faith. Ezekial, Haym's older son, eventually moved to New Orleans, where he worked for the New Orleans branch of the United States Bank. He died in 1822.

Haym M., the younger son, like his father, opened a mercantile business in New York. In 1844 Haym M. quit that business and put all of his efforts into trying to collect repayment on all the money his father had loaned to the Continental Congress between 1781 and 1784 to help pay for the Revolutionary War. The amount in question was $353,744. In addition, Haym M. stated that his father had advanced money to Robert Morris for $211,000, as well as $92,000 for additional loans to the Congress. There was also a balance of $10,000 loaned to the Spanish Ambassador, as well as loans to others in the government, including James Madison.

There is still in existence a letter written by Haym M. Salomon from New York on January 22, 1830 requesting repayment to his father's estate. It was written "To His Excellency James Madison" and signed, "With the greatest respect, allow me to subscribe myself—Your grateful friend and servant— Haym M. Salomon."

Although these claims made by Haym M. concerning his father's service and loans to the Continental Congress were considered by the United States Congress at least ten times between 1848 and 1926, and it was noted that James

Madison had testified to the loans before Congress, no money was ever voted to be returned to the Salomon heirs. Although the Congress voted to erect a statue of Salomon, that was never done either.

Haym Salomon was a true patriot and supporter of his adopted nation, but he has never been given sufficient credit for his heroic financial transactions. This lack of recognition has still not been rectified by the United States Congress or by any sitting president. Today there are still descendants of Haym Salomon who could in fact be his heirs—if not to his fortune, at least to his excellent reputation.

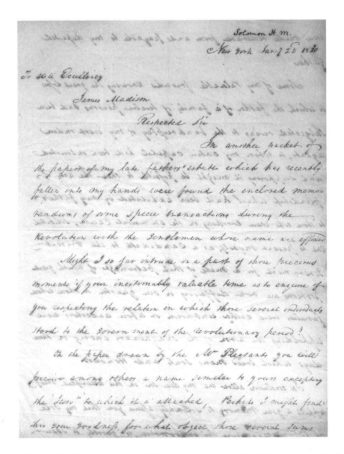

Letter from Haym M. Salomon, son of Haym Salomon, to President James Madison, dated January 22, 1820, in which he documents his father's claim of money due to the family for having helped finance the Revolution.

Moses Michael Hays

A Boston Businessman

Moses Michael Hays of Boston. Hays was a founder of the Bank of Boston and an active member of the Masons, along with Paul Revere, who was in his lodge.

MOSES Michael Hays was born on May 9, 1739, in New York City. In his early career, he worked in the trading and shipping business of his father, Judah Hays. In 1768, he married Rachel Myers, the sister of New York silversmith Myer Myers. He was active in the Jewish community, supporting the first American Jewish congregation, Shearith Israel. His sister, Reyna Hays, was married to the Reverend Isaac Touro of Newport, Rhode Island, and by 1768, Moses and his wife were also living in Newport. His business ventures in Newport were unsuccessful, and he went bankrupt in 1771. Over the next decade he moved his family part-time to Boston, and in 1782 he made Boston his permanent home.

In Boston, Moses Michael Hays made a full recovery in the business world. He became an insurance broker, a commission salesman, a dealer in bills of exchange in London, and a real estate agent, all at the same time, out of his office at 68 State Street. It was not long before he was a very wealthy man.

He received and wrote hundreds of pieces of correspondence over the course of his lifetime. Some of them were personal letters to family and friends; others concerned business transactions. He corresponded with Michael Gratz of Philadelphia, for example, about a business transaction that linked Hays and Gratz to Abraham Sarzedos of Savannah, Georgia, and Isaac Da Costa of Charleston, South Carolina, in the importation of products from the island of Curaçao.

*   *   *

Moses and Rachel had seven children, six of whom lived to be adults. The family lived in a fine brick house with fifteen rooms, thirty-one windows, a store and a library; it was called by Hays's friends "a mansion of peace." In this house, he received many important guests, including Harrison Gray Otis, a senator and mayor of Boston, and Thomas H. Perkins, the railroad entrepreneur and philanthropist. His sister, Reyna, by then a widow, also lived in Hays's home.

Moses was known to be a generous host to all he met, rich or poor. One person to receive his hospitality was the grandfather of Louisa May Alcott, who wrote:

> Many indigent families were fed pretty regularly from his table. They would come especially after his frequent dinner parties, and were sure to be made welcome, not to the crumbs only, but to ampler portions of the food that might be left.
>
> Always, on Saturday, he expected a number of friends to dine with him. A full-length table was always spread, and loaded with the luxuries of the season; and he loved to see it surrounded by a few regular visitors and others especially invited. My father…seldom failed to dine at Mr. Hays on Saturday, and often took me with him; for he was sure I should meet refined company there.
>
> Both Uncle and Aunt Hays (for so I called them) were fond of children, particularly of me; and I was permitted to stay with them several days, and even weeks, together. And I can never forget, not merely their kind, but their conscientious care of me. I was the child of Christian parents, and they took especial pains that I should lose nothing of religious training so long as I was permitted to abide with them. Every night, I was required, on going to bed, to repeat my Christian hymns and prayer to them, or else to an excellent Christian servant woman who lived with them many years. I witnessed their religious exercises—their fastings and their prayers—and was made to feel that they worshipped the Unseen Almighty and All-merciful One. Of course I grew up without any prejudice against Jews—or any other religionists, because they did not believe as my father and mother believed.

Boston had no Jewish community in Moses's time. The Hays family was one of several that continued to support Newport's Touro Synagogue and remained an active part of Newport's Jewish community. In his personal life, Hays had regular religious worship at his home in Boston. He also saw to it

New york June 4. 1765

Juse the freedom to request you will Forward The Inclosd For Mr. abm Sayedas to Georgia With some care as it is of Moment, and should there be no Immediate offer for Georgia, please to put in under Cover to Mr. Isaac Da Costa at Charlestown & Forward it by first vessell, with telling Mr. Da Costa, That it is my Desire he will Forward it with Care ferport, you have Also here Coverd a Letter for Mr. Miranda its Contents no doubt he will acquaint you with, am informed you Intend Embarqueing with him for Curracoa, from whence shall be Glad of your Correspondence as have wrote him. Wishing you a safe passage & every other Wish to promote your prosperity

Dear sr. Yr most hble servant

Moses M. Hays

Letter from Moses Michael Hays, regarding business relations with Jewish merchants in other colonial towns, including Mr. Abraham Sarzedas of Georgia and Mr. Miranda and M. Isaac da Costa of Charleston. There were many business transactions conducted between Jewish people in the colonies, the Caribbean islands, and Great Britain.

that his children were educated in Hebrew and learned to live as traditional Jews. They had a fine resource to call upon, as the Hays personal library had over twenty Hebrew volumes.

The family bible was inscribed with Moses Michael Hays's Hebrew name, Moshe Ben Yuhudah. Its covers inside are of marbled paper. His Torah was printed in 1725 in Amsterdam, and it has leather covers. Both volumes are now in the Wyner Museum of Temple Israel, in Boston.

Moses Michael Hays helped establish the financial stability of the city of Boston by helping to charter the Massachusetts Bank, which eventually became the First National Bank of Boston. He was one of nine men who put the money together to open the bank's doors for business on July 5, 1784. He was the bank's first depositor and also the first to withdraw any funds.

Hays was also among the petitioners for a charter for the Massachusetts Mutual Fire Insurance Company, one of the first companies of its type in New England. He became involved, as a merchant, in the China trade, becoming an investor in the first ship to trade with the Chinese for silks, teas, and porcelain. That ship, the *Empress of China,* sailed in 1784. Hays also invested in ships that sailed from the Northeast in America to the Northwest to pick up the fur pelts wanted by the Chinese in trade for their silks, spices, teas, porcelain, etc. He also saw the need to bond and insure those vessels engaged in the China trade.

Hays was involved with Free Masonry. In 1769, he was the Master of King David's Lodge in New York City, and his brother-in-law, silversmith Myer Myers, was the Senior Warden under him. When he moved to Newport and then to Boston, Moses continued to support the Masons, and in Boston he served as the Grand Master of the Grand Lodge of Massachusetts. This time it was Paul Revere, another silversmith, who served as Deputy Grand Master under him, from 1788 to 1792. Hays also served as Deputy Inspector General of Masonry for North America. Hays's Grand Mason's apron is still housed at the Masonic Lodge in Boston. It was made of lambskin with silk ties.

Another remarkable contribution Moses Michael Hays made, which is of special interest to historians and silver collectors, was to bring together two of the most important silversmiths of the time, Myer Myers and Paul Revere. Moses was related to Myer Myers by marriage, and he was associated with both men through the Masons. Eventually he put the two craftsmen together personally. This happened when two of his daughters, Judith and Sally Hays, married two

Sterling silver teapot made by Paul Revere for Moses Michael Hays, the only Jew for whom he ever worked. Revere made other silver pieces for the Hays family as well.

of Myers's sons, Samuel Myers and Moses Mears Myers, respectively. For these two unions, Hays had Paul Revere make silver wedding presents, in the form of sets of teaspoons and a teapot.

The Hays family was the only Jewish family that Revere worked for. He made them a teapot in 1783, a cream pot in 1784, sauceboats in 1790, and drinking goblets in 1792. At various times he also made them ragout spoons (large spoons with which to eat stews) and several sets of tablespoons and teaspoons. There is a set of twelve fluted-bowl spoons, made by Revere for Moses Michael Hays in 1787, now in the John Quincy Adams State Drawing Room at the State Department in Washington, D.C. Also at the State Department is Revere's sugar basket, made the same year for Hays, bearing the initials "MRH," for Moses and Rachel Hays. The name Hays appears twenty-five times in the accounting daybooks of Paul Revere's silversmithing business.

* * *

Moses Michael Hays's portrait was painted by Gilbert Stuart, the man who painted portraits of Presidents George Washington, John Adams, and Thomas Jefferson. A copy of the original, made in 1873 by E.M. Carpenter, hangs today in the Masonic Temple in Boston.

Hays died intestate in 1805 at the age of 66. His wife, Rachel, survived him. He is buried along with other family members at Newport's Colonial Jewish Cemetery. His obituary stated that he was possessed of a strong intellect, that there was a vigor in his conception of men and things, and that he feared no man but loved all.

His son, Judah, inherited most of the Hays family wealth. Judah was the first Jew elected to public office in Boston in 1805 and he was a founder of the prestigious Boston Athenaeum.

Moses Michael Hays's talents for charity, service, and business success have survived to the present time, as there are many of his descendants still making contributions to American society today.

The Cohens
and the Ettings

*They Brought Jewish Society
to Baltimore*

*Miniature portrait of Rachel Gratz Etting, second
wife of Salomon Etting, by American portraitist
Thomas Sully. Rachel was the only daughter
of Barnard Gratz.*

THE Jewish community of Baltimore, Maryland, was established very late. Unlike other cities in the colonies, Baltimore did not attract Jews. For that matter, all of Maryland was inhospitable to the Jews. It was largely a Catholic community, one that required an oath of faith in Jesus Christ in order to practice certain professions or hold public office. This law stayed on the books until well into the nineteenth century.

There were a few Jews who tried to live in Maryland, such as Jacob Lumbrezo, who came from Portugal in 1656, but no real community existed for almost 150 years after that. Lumbrezo was actually accused of blasphemy and was prosecuted, although he was released and in fact prospered in Maryland before his death in 1665. His will indicates that he was able to acquire land and a modest estate, working at various times as a folk doctor, a farmer, and an innkeeper. Another brave entrepreneur, Benjamin Levy, came to Maryland and advertised the opening of his shop in the *Maryland Journal* and the *Baltimore Advertiser* in 1773.

But it was not until the arrival of two important families, the Ettings of York, Pennsylvania, and the Cohens from Richmond, Virginia, that Baltimore can be said to have had a viable Jewish community.

In 1759, Shinah Solomon, the daughter of Joseph Solomon of Lancaster, Pennsylvania, married Elijah Etting, a native of Frankfurt, Germany, who had

J. Marx Etting as a child. The Etting family was involved in the American China trade. Pieces of the porcelain they brought to America are now in the Philadelphia Museum of Art.

arrived in York, Pennsylvania that year. After her husband died on July 3, 1778, Mrs. Etting and her children moved to Baltimore, where she supported her family by running a boarding house. She was successful, and she was characterized by one of her neighbors as "always in spirits, full of frolic and glee." This happy spirit can be seen in the portrait painted by Charles Peale Polk, a nephew of the artist Charles Wilson Peale. Mrs. Etting was the matriarch of one of the most prominent families in Baltimore, some of whose descendants still live there today.

The Etting family also had connections by marriage to other important Jewish families in early America. One of these families was the Gratz family of Philadelphia; Reuben Etting married Rachel Gratz, the daughter of Barnard. Both the Simon family and the Gratz family were instrumental in helping to open up the western part of Pennsylvania and in promoting the further expansion into Ohio and Kentucky.

It was another widow, Judith Cohen, who brought the other prominent Jewish family to Baltimore, when she came with her six sons and one daughter in about 1784, after her husband, Israel I. Cohen, died suddenly at the age of

Salomon Etting of Baltimore. A prominent merchant, Etting was also a shochet, *or ritual slaughterer of kosher meat, and an abolitionist who spoke against slavery. He was also a proponent of religious freedom.*

forty-three. She made this move because she wanted her children to be educated in a college that the Maryland legislature ruled would be open to students of all religions. This same right of education had been denied to the Cohen children in Virginia because they were Jewish.

The tradition continued. In Maryland, the Cohens were patriots and humanitarians, campaigning for religious emancipation. In this effort, they were joined by the Ettings, who also felt a responsibility to stand up for the rights of Jews and others to hold public office in the state of Maryland in all its counties. Salomon Etting spearheaded the movement to remove the requirement of an oath professing belief in the Christian religion. It took twenty-nine years for this law to be changed, but eventually it was changed, with the help of a state legislator, Thomas Kennedy.

Both families prospered. Influential in banking, real estate, railroads, and financial lotteries, the Cohens and the Ettings became an important force in the economic and political life of Baltimore, where they enjoyed an aristocratic life style as wealthy and successful members of Maryland society.

There were six Cohen brothers. The most well known was Jacob I. Cohen, who organized a successful lottery business. Baltimore lotteries were very important, providing the way to fund public buildings and monuments, and although not all lotteries were legitimate, Jacob Cohen's lottery was highly respected. Jacob was also president of the Baltimore city council at one time and the secretary-treasurer of the city school system. He was also a director of the Baltimore and Ohio Railway.

Talented in many areas, Dr. Joshua Cohen, in addition to being one of the first ear specialists in America, took time to study geology and mineralogy. He became a professor of these subjects at the University of Maryland. He was a founder of the Hebrew Hospital in Baltimore. He also developed his own Hebrew library, still considered one of the finest Hebrew libraries in America. Consisting of over three hundred volumes, it was catalogued in 1887 by Cyrus Adler and it is now owned by the Dropsie College of Philadelphia.

Benjamin I. Cohen was a prominent banker who was one of the founders of the Baltimore Stock Exchange. Jacob, Philip, and Mendes Cohen, along with Samuel Etting, helped defend Fort McHenry against the British during the War of 1812.

In spite of their influence in the civic and social life of Baltimore, the Cohens and the Ettings were very private families who tended to keep to themselves in many areas of life. This was particularly true of their religious practices. (There was no real Jewish community in that city when they first arrived, but even

The "Jew Bill," which gave Jews in Maryland the right to participate in the political forum of the state. This bill of 1819 was approved many years later than those same rights were granted to all by the Constitution.

after more Jewish families came to Baltimore, the Cohens and Ettings did not socialize with the newcomers, many of whom they considered to be undereducated immigrant peddlers. It was not until 1829 that the first Jewish congregation was chartered, after which the Jewish community began to function for the benefit of all who wanted to join.)

Until then, both families maintained their own private religious services and minyans (the ten men necessary for communal prayers) at their homes for over fifty years after coming to Baltimore. They conducted marriages and other ceremonies at home, and both families had private burial plots. They even circumcised their boys at home, themselves. They also slaughtered their own meat, adhering to strict ritual to keep it kosher, and Salomon Etting was one of the first native-born Americans to be licensed as a ritual slaughterer (shochet) of kosher meat.

The Ettings and the Cohens had an elegant life style. They purchased lavish furnishings for their homes and gorgeous silver plate for their tables. They had their portraits painted by the best known artists of the day, like Rembrandt Peale and John Wesley Jarvis. Today, most of those portraits, along with hundreds of pieces of silver, furniture, glass, ceramics, and textiles comprise a major part of the colonial collection at the Maryland Historical Society in Baltimore.

Known for the high positions they held socially, in business life, and politically during the early history of Maryland, the Cohens and Ettings are best known for the many contributions they made as activists and for their many philanthropic contributions to Baltimore, to Maryland, and to America.

Gershom Mendes Seixas

*Spiritual Leader
for Shearith Israel*

Reverend Gershom Mendes Seixas. Rev. Seixas led the first Jewish congregation in America, Shearith Israel in New York, for forty-six years. He sat on the founding board of Kings College (Columbia University) in New York, and served as clergyman at the inauguration of President George Washington.

ONE of the most important spiritual leaders in early American history was Gershom Mendes Seixas, a third-generation Jewish-American New Yorker who served his community as the leader of Shearith Israel for forty-eight years, including the years surrounding the American Revolution.

The history of Shearith Israel goes back to 1654, when New York was still Dutch New Amsterdam. The oldest Jewish congregation in the United States, it was started by the original twenty-three Jews who came to New York from Recife, Brazil. It was a Sephardic synagogue in the Spanish-Portuguese style, and was originally called the Mill Street Synagogue. The congregation still exists today. It is now in its fifth location, on Central Park West, which includes parts of the original structure from Mill Street. They are housed in the Little Synagogue in Shearith Israel's present home. Many important families have played a part in Shearith Israel's history, as contributors and as leaders, and one of the most prominent figures in the history of the congregation was Reverend Gershom Mendes Seixas.

This man was not a rabbi in the European sense of the word. He was not a "haham," or a man who has been given instruction orally, in the traditions passed from learned man to learned man. Instead, he was a "minister" respected by both Jews and non-Jews alike for his spirituality and his ability to communicate. He held the devoted attention of his congregation for almost half a century. He also invited members of the local Episcopal community to attend Shearith Israel's services. In his desire to make Judaism more accessible to all, he suggested to Shearith Israel that the English and Spanish languages be used to supplement Hebrew in books and in prayers.

As the leader of New York's Shearith Israel, Reverend Seixas represented the Jewish community to the general community, not only in New York, but in all of America. In 1754 he sat on the founding board of King's College in New York, which in 1784 became known as Columbia University. That post involved important decisions concerning education, and it also involved an interfaith exchange of ideas and activities between Reverend Seixas and clergy from other faiths.

Reverend Seixas took an active role in the American Revolution. When the non-importation petitions were being circulated, demanding of England that there be no taxation without representation, Reverend Seixas saw to it that many members of his congregation and the Jewish community signed. When the British entered New York City in 1779, Gershom Seixas and many members of the congregation (most of whom were far from loyal to the British throne) left the city and sought safe haven in Philadelphia. Seixas took with him much of Shearith Israel's religious property, including the Torahs, to save them from British hands, since the British had already burned one of their Torahs. In Philadelphia, he helped restructure the Jewish community and helped organize the building of Philadelphia's first synagogue, Mikveh Israel. He contributed a washing bowl and a pair of candlesticks to the new edifice when it opened in 1783. After the Revolution, he returned to New York and to Shearith Israel.

In 1789, he took part in the inauguration of President George Washington. The ceremony was in New York, and Reverend Seixas was one of fourteen clergymen invited to participate. This honor illustrated the new country's high regard for Seixas's role in the Jewish community at that time. Seixas was known affectionately as "Patriot Rabbi."

Other members of the Seixas family were noteworthy also. Gershom's brother, Benjamin Seixas, was a trader and merchant who became a Yankee privateer. That means he used his ship to attack British ships and take the much-needed cargo that had been withheld from the American colonies by the British. In 1792, Benjamin, along with his business partner, Ezekiel Hart, were among the founders of one of the most important financial institutions in America, the New York Stock Exchange, although Ezekiel Hart did not

Chatham Square Cemetery, New York, the oldest Jewish burial ground in America. Many Jewish Revolutionary War patriots and many seventeenth- and eighteenth-century Jewish New Yorkers are buried here. The cemetery can still be visited today.

sign the Buttonwood Document that formed the Exchange under the Buttonwood Tree.

Gershom's son, David Seixas, liked to experiment with new ideas, and he helped to introduce daguerrotype, the precursor to photography, in America. He also made printing ink and sealing wax, and even operated a beer brewery at one time. But the contribution for which David Seixas is most famous was the Institution for the Deaf and Dumb, in Philadelphia. He began this institution by taking four or five such handicapped children into his home at a time. There he fed them, clothed, them, and taught them to communicate so that they could return to their families and to society with new abilities. David convinced the state of Pennsylvania that his organization should be maintained and supported financially.

David was also in the pottery business, manufacturing Queensware pottery in Philadelphia, according to an advertisement in the *Niles Register* in Baltimore in 1817. One of the products that he made was a pitcher molded in a diamond relief pattern with a rounded body that is glazed in green. In the front of the pitcher, under the spout, is a circle with a portrait of David's father, Gershom Mendes Seixas, who died shortly after the pitcher was made.

When Reverend Seixas died, he was buried at Chatham Square Cemetery. His tombstone is in the shape of an obelisk, signifying his importance in the community, as is George Washington's monument in Washington, D.C. He was one of the most beloved and respected ministers, not only within his congregation, but throughout the American colonies and the newborn nation.

Gravestone of Rev. Gershom Mendes Seixas, in the form of an obelisk. During the colonial period in America, obelisks usually marked the graves of very important members of a community.

The Moses Myers Family

A Family Home in Norfolk, for Many Generations

Moses Myers. Myers was a merchant in Norfolk, Virginia, where his family was the only Jewish family in 1790, although he continued to pay dues to his synagogue, Shearith Israel in New York. In Norfolk he had land consecrated for his family's private cemetery. Portrait by Gilbert Stuart, who also did portraits of George Washington.

MOSES Myers was born in 1752 in New York City. His father, Hyam Myers had arrived from Amsterdam in the late 1740s. Shortly after arriving in New York, Hyam Myers became an employee of the first Jewish congregation in America, the Spanish-Portuguese synagogue, Shearith Israel in New York, as a shochet, or ritual slaughterer. Hyam did this job until he was able to establish himself as a trader, exporting goods to Canada, to which he eventually migrated. In June of 1751, Hyam married Rachel, the daughter of Moses Louzada, whose family had lived in New York as early as 1689.

Moses was their eldest child. The first twenty years of his life were relatively uneventful, spent within the boundaries of New York City. His story really begins in 1773, just before the American Revolutionary War, when Moses, at the age of twenty-one, became a junior partner in the firm of Isaac Moses & Company in New York. Isaac Moses was in turn a partner of the merchant Samuel Myers of Amsterdam. This business had offices in Amsterdam and in New York, as traders of English and European goods. During the British blockade of North America, the partners opened another office on the Caribbean Island of St. Eustatius. There they helped supply the hard-pressed American patriots with badly needed goods that had been withheld by the British. Unfortunately, the British invaded St. Eustatius and confiscated the partners' goods during the Revolution, which sent the partners into bankruptcy, and

Eliza Myers, wife of Moses Myers. Originally from the Judah family of Montreal, Canada, Eliza oversaw the beautiful home in Norfolk she shared with her husband and children. The house still stands today, with most of its belongings intact.

both the firm and Moses's job quietly dissolved.

At that point, Moses decided to travel to the Southern part of the United States to begin his career again. In one of his diary entries he wrote, "In Virginia, money is yet to be made, as it is in both Charleston and Richmond."

Myers's primary goal here was to find a location where he could accumulate "a modest fortune." After visiting the most important Southern cities at that time—Charleston, South Carolina; Savannah, Georgia; Baltimore, Maryland; Richmond, Virginia; and Norfolk, Virginia—he chose Norfolk for its spacious harbor.

A painting by Benjamin Henry Latrobe shows how Norfolk looked in the 1790s. Looking down from Botetort Street, the painting shows the many ships in the harbor, docked along Main Street. We also see the nearby wharves of Portsmouth, Virginia. Norfolk at that time was famous among visitors from near and far, as it rivaled all other seaports in America. It is no wonder that Moses chose to settle in this Tidewater area, especially since the State of Virginia actively supported its budding economy.

Just before this move, however, Moses improved both his own fortune and his domestic life by marrying Elizabeth, or Eliza, a member of the prominent Canadian Judah family from Montreal. This was the second marriage for Eliza, who had been married as a teenager to a frontiersman, Chapman Abraham. Chapman had followed the French Canadian trade routes up the St. Lawrence seaway and through the Great Lakes to become the first Jewish settler in 1761 in the area that we today call Detroit, Michigan. But Chapman died in 1783, when Eliza was only twenty-four years of age. She was pregnant at the time of her first husband's death, but the baby was stillborn. In 1787, on March 22, the eve of Passover, Eliza married again, this time to Moses Myers in New York.

At that time, Moses once again became a partner to a Samuel Myers. But this Samuel Myers was from Richmond, Virginia. He was the son of Myer Myers, the well-known New York colonial Jewish silversmith. The two men rented a store in Norfolk, and in 1787, Eliza and Moses packed their belongings and boarded the schooner *Sincerity*, bound for their new Virginia home.

On August 1, the partners, Samuel and Moses, issued a formal announcement of their store, dealing in "naval supplies, corn, beeswax, deer skins, tobacco, and lumber, of all sorts in abundance, very good and very cheap." Business prospered, and soon Moses was involved in a growing import-export business on an even larger scale. His family began growing, too; during their married life, Moses and Eliza gave birth to twelve children, nine of whom lived to be adults: John, Samuel, Adeline, Myer, Frederick, Augusta, Abram, Hyam, and Mary Georgia.

Norfolk's post-Revolutionary history (1793–1880) vividly illustrates the volatile nature of any community whose existence depends upon maritime commerce. During the nineteenth century, Norfolk's populace differed in composition from that of its neighboring agricultural communities. This was a city of merchants and a city full of sailors, as well as the wharves and the ships there assuring a continuing prosperity, and life was hectic, very different from the slower-paced Southern plantation style. As Thomas Wertenbaker notes:

> They were first of all practical, keen businessmen, lacking the taste for political life, the urge for study, and the philosophical view, which the plantations systems fostered in their neighbors. Norfolk produced no Washington, no Jefferson, no Madison.

In spite of the heat and occasional outbreaks of malaria, Norfolk was a vibrant, bustling port. As Anne Ritson, a British traveler, described in verse in 1809:

> *The town is built upon the shore,*
> *In length about a mile or more;*
> *Quite to the shore the vessels ride*
> *All is taken in their stride.*

In 1790, as Norfolk became prosperous, so did Moses. He became Virginia's agent for the wealthy Philadelphian, Stephen Girard, who founded the Girard

Bank in Pennsylvania. Besides being Girard's agent, Moses became the owner of two schooners, the *Eliza*, named after his wife, and the *Paragon*.

With his wealth well secured, in September 1791 Moses purchased a large lot on which he erected the magnificent Georgian townhouse that still bears his name today. Completed in 1792, with later additions to follow, the house was considered one of the finest brick homes to be built in Norfolk. It took only one year to be built, and Moses furnished it with the treasures he had obtained from his worldwide import-export trading establishment. The house was located at the corner of Freemason and Catherine Streets, six blocks from the harbor and about six blocks from his business in Market Square. From the side of the porch, Myers could keep an eye out for the ships that came and went from Norfolk in his name.

The house was built in what was then the geographical center of the city. The building of this house coincided with the building of Moses's reputation as both a successful merchant prince and an active leader in Norfolk's expanding affairs. He served as a city council member, and when the Bank of Richmond opened its Norfolk branch in 1792, Moses was appointed the superintendent. Two years later, in 1794, he became Mercantile Agent for the French government. He was also the representive for The Netherlands and Denmark in the Batavian market. He became the President of the Common Council in Norfolk, and like most of the gentlemen in his circumstances, he was commissioned as an officer in the Virginia militia, serving in the 54th Regiment as a captain in 1798 and in 1800 as a major.

A firsthand account of Moses Myers's reputation is given by Mereau de St. Mercy, a Frenchman who had fled with his family from the horrors of the Reign of Terror of the French Revolution. In his account of his family's travels in the United States, *Voyage Aux Etats-Unis de l'Amerique, 1793–1798,* he wrote the following: "Business matters took us to the home of Moses Myers, a Norfolk merchant, whose praises had been sung to us even before we disembarked. The excellent food, the sight of the fond mother, who even suckled a lusty infant during the meal, his four pretty children—everything charmed us."

The Myers house was built in the Georgian style of architecture. The term Georgian refers to the period of English history from the reign of George I, beginning in 1720, through the reign of George IV. This style, originally derived from both Greek and Roman classical architecture, was reintroduced by the Italian architect Andrea Palladio. Using the elements of Greek and Roman architecture, including decorated classical columns, arches, and pediments—the style achieves an effect of great elegance and simplicity through the careful selection of proportions and the balanced repetition of its characteristic

The Moses Myers House. Built in 1792, the house remained in the Myers family until 1930. Today it is open to the public.

decorative features. For example, the outside of the Myers's home has strong classical pediments or decoration applied on the outside of the house, such as the rounded window-tops of the attic and the classical columns. The overall impression of this building is one of restrained elegance. The Georgian style of this house was inspired by the Scottish-born architect Robert Adam, who worked in the late eighteenth-century classical style.

It is important to note that in houses that are referred to as Georgian, the interiors were even more elaborate than the exteriors. The main entry into this house is from the side of the structure, which was typical of the Southern townhouse. In the entry hall, there is the original heart-of-pine wooden flooring that also exists throughout the house. It was laid with random widths, using hand-cut nails in the tradition of that time. The hall extends across the whole front of the house, rather than going through the house front to back, which was more typical of Southern homes. This arrangement permitted three entrances, one on each side and one in the middle. This entry hall, like all the other rooms in the house, is exceptionally well proportioned, with a high ceiling and generous windows that permit natural light to penetrate deep into the rooms. Venetian blinds, slat curtains, and working outside shutters provide sun control in the summer and help to reduce heat loss in the winter. With such large windows, there were probably also fine views of the water. The entry was called the "Passage Below," according to an inventory made in 1819.

In the parlor there is a fireplace with an elegant mantle, made in Philadelphia to complement the balanced design of the architect, Robert Adam. In the parlor are oil portraits of Moses and Eliza Myers painted on poplar wood panels. They still hang in their original five-inch gilt wood frames. They are the work of Gilbert Stuart, 1755–1828, who also painted President George Washington's portrait. Judging from the age of the sitters—Moses appears to be about fifty and Eliza in her early forties—these portraits were probably painted during Stuart's eight-year stay in Philadelphia, late in his life, just before he moved to Boston in 1805.

Portrait painters constituted a large artistic force at the turn of the nineteenth century. Many newly affluent middle-class citizens, such as the Myers family of New York, desired some tangible evidence of their business successes. Moses and Eliza Myers had created a relatively luxurious life through their ability to take advantage of the burgeoning import-export trade in Norfolk, and Stuart's painting reveals their confident prosperity without excessive movements, identifiable moods, or lavish furnishings.

The windows in the parlor, as in the other rooms in the house, have interior window shutters that fold back into the walls, so that they are concealed

Dining room of the Myers house. The room is filled with mahogany furniture in the Hepplewhite style, Chinese-export porcelain in the Fitzhugh pattern, and many pieces of crystal and silver. Beneath the table is floor cloth made to resemble the marbleized floors of eighteenth-century Great Britain.

when not in use. Closed, they helped control heat and light and provide privacy and security.

The dining room chamber is one of the handsomest of its kind left standing in the South, and it is furnished exclusively with pieces original to the house. The dining room was a later addition to the house in 1797. The Washington, D.C. architect Benjamin Latrobe has been associated with this addition, but there is no documentary evidence to connect him with this house other than the fact that he happened to be in the city at the time it was built. Benjamin Latrobe was also one of the architects for the Capitol of the United States.

The twelve chairs accompanying the table, the two arm chairs, and the other side chairs are crafted of mahogany in what was known as shield-back Hepplewhite style. The Hepplewhite style was brought to America in the form of his style book called *The Cabinet Makers and Upholsterer's Guide,* published in 1794 by his wife, Alice, after Hepplewhite's death in England in 1786. The seats of the chair are covered in actual horsehair that is woven tightly, hard to sit on, but easy to clean. Also in the room is a handsome tall Sheffield oval tea

Music room of the Myers house. The Myers family loved music; they kept many instruments and owned one of the largest collections of music in all the colonies.

urn with golden borders. The base is square with ball feet. The cover has a ball finial. It was made in England between 1790 and 1795 and was used to keep water for coffee or tea hot for up to an hour.

There is a music room that contains many furnishings brought by Moses and Eliza Myers when they moved to Norfolk from New York in 1787. There is a mahogany pianoforte with satinwood inlay and a decoration of painted flowers above the keyboard. The range is only five octaves.

Musical education and enjoyment were an integral part of the Myers's household. All the members of the family participated in playing or singing selections from their musical library, and the Myers music collection was one of the largest family collections in the United States. There are thirty-one bound volumes, containing musical scores for harp, pianoforte, violin, flute, and clarinet, as well as voice. The pieces include works by Bach, Beethoven, Brahms, Handel, Haydn, Mozart, and the Scottish poet, Robert Burns.

Above the fireplace mantle in this room hangs a portrait of the Myers's son, John, then in his twenty-first year, painted in 1808 by Thomas Sully, the American portraitist. This portrait of John Myers depicts wealth and social standing through a display of telling details: a gloved hand, elaborate drapery, and an upholstered chair.

In addition to the music library, the Myers family had a sizable book collection containing approximately a thousand volumes. A study undertaken mainly to list the titles in the Myers's family collection concluded that their library was typical of those owned by the intelligent upper-class merchants and planters of their day. It included, for example, works by Shakespeare, Alexander Pope, John Locke, Homer, and George Washington. The books covered a wide range of subjects: philosophy, political science, history, literature, natural science, geography, and anatomy; there were also books of religious treatises and three bibles, including one Jewish Bible. There are works written in seven major languages—English, French, Italian, German, Spanish, Hebrew, and Portuguese.

The Myers's kitchen was equipped with bowls of wood, butter paddles, sugar snippers to cut the cane from the Caribbean Islands, and a mortar and pestle for grinding herbs and spices. The women prepared meals in the kitchen in a large fireplace. Copper pots were used to cook the rice, beans, peas, and other staples that were standard fare of the times. There was one family cook and one scullery maid who tended to the Myers's family. Some of the family's herbs, vegetables, and fruits were grown in the family's garden plots beside and behind the house.

There were six other rooms in the house, including four bedrooms upstairs. The master suite still contains Moses's clothes, including coats, hats, breeches, and waistcoats, as well as a sea chest, a sextant, and a traveling lap desk. From Eliza, we have dresses, a shawl, and a miniature watercolor-on-ivory portrait of Moses given to her as a wedding brooch. It is framed in gold with blue enamel and seed pearls, and a lock of Moses's hair is tucked in the back of the case. There is her candle stand and candle snuffer and a cradle intended for the children when they were small. There are also, elsewhere in the house, the horse pistols that Moses kept in holsters on either side of his saddle when he traveled, to protect himself against highway robbers.

In such a prosperous family, the education of the children was an important matter. The boys attended the newly opened Norfolk Academy, while the girls were tutored by the best teachers at home. The girls learned literature, music, and the arts, as well as the culinary skills of women of the household.

John, the eldest son, was trained in his father's business at age twenty-one, in 1808, and on May, 1809, was given full partnership in the firm, which became Moses Myers & Son. To expand his business education, John was sent abroad, and he eventually opened a branch office in Baltimore, Maryland.

The second son, Samuel, was enrolled in 1808 into one of the first colleges chartered in America, College of William and Mary at Williamsburg, Virginia. Samuel was the first person of Jewish faith to matriculate there. He studied law for two years and then went to work with a Richmond lawyer. Samuel married, while in Richmond, Louise Marx, the daughter of his father's old friend, Joseph Marx.

Only three of the Myers's children married—Samuel, Myer, and Augusta—and Samuel was the only one to have offspring. The two sons, Samuel and Myer, married sisters from Richmond. Samuel married Louise Marx and Myer married Judith Marx. Augusta married Philip I. Cohen of Baltimore in 1826.

Religion played an important part in Myers family life, although when Moses and Eliza arrived in Norfolk in 1787, they were the city's only Jewish family. There was not a rabbi, a synagogue, a minyan of ten men, or a community of Jewish people. There was no one else in the city with whom to share their religious values or faith. For this reason, Moses to continued to support his family's synagogue in New York, Shearith Israel, with annual dues and contributions. He also maintained close personal ties to Jewish friends, such as the Gratz family of Philadelphia, the Cohens of Baltimore, and the Marxes and Myers of Richmond. Moses also bought and consecrated a burial plot in Norfolk for his family to be buried in the Jewish faith. So even though Moses and his family were isolated from formal Judaism, they remained interested in preserving their ancestral faith.

That tradition continued into the next generation. In 1818, Samuel Myers, the second son, became actively involved in establishing a boarding school for Jewish children. None of the Myers children married out of their Jewish faith. Today none of the Myers descendants practice Judaism in Norfolk.

Moses Myers had an active and successful career both in business and in public service. He was a world-wide merchant who traded freely with many countries. In the first decade of the nineteenth century, Moses had corresponded with practically every major seaport on both sides of the Atlantic ocean. In addition to his business concerns, he was appointed to a diplomatic position for Denmark in 1812 and to one for Holland in 1819. President John Quincy Adams appointed Myers Collector of Customs for the Port of Norfolk in 1828.

But success did not last for his entire life. The War of 1812 between the United States and Great Britain had a major impact on Moses Myers, for the heavy trading embargo acts of 1807 to 1815 caused him to lose his entire fortune. As dire times approached with the end of the war, Moses was forced into bankruptcy in 1818. A financial cloud was to hang over Moses's head for the rest of his life. His creditors, however, realized the beauty of the Myers house and its contents and agreed to let him and his family keep their home, intact. The Myers family continued to live in that home for five generations.

Business reversals were not the only problem to plague Moses Myers and his family. The Myers family had their share of happiness, but they also suffered their share of grief, beginning with the loss of three children in infancy.

Their son, Samuel, came home one day to find that his father had been struck on the head and pushed down by an angry business associate. Samuel furiously sought out the assailant at his place of work, pulled out a gun, and killed the man. Samuel was arrested for manslaughter, and although he was allowed out on bail, he and his family had to wait for a whole year for the return of a "Not Guilty" verdict based on the finding that Samuel had been defending his father's life. The family was totally distraught by the tragic affair, and the outpouring of concern and sympathy for Moses and his family was overwhelming, including letters from President James Madison and the Gratz brothers (Barnard and Michael) of Philadelphia.

In 1821, Moses and Eliza's son Abram died suddenly at the young age of twenty-one; and and in 1822, his brother Henry died at sea, still wearing the naval uniform he had worn to fight in the War of 1812. Eliza, their mother, was unable to conquer her grief. She went home to Montreal to visit her family and there in 1823, she died. She was greatly mourned by her family and friends.

At one time, Moses Myers was considered one of the fifteen wealthiest men in the United States, with over six million dollars in net worth. He lost it all and died in poverty. But the brick home that he constructed in 1792 still stands today in Norfolk at the corner of Freemason and Bank.

During the Confederacy, the Myers home served as the British Consulate. (The family kept possession of the house, but allowed the British to fly their flag.) Many famous people have visited the house over the years, including Stephen Decatur, Lafayette, James Monroe, Henry Clay, General Winfield Scott, President Taft, and President Theodore Roosevelt.

It is remarkable that this house remained in the possession of one family for five generations; it is also extraordinary that over seventy-five percent of its present furnishings date back to the original Moses Myers family. We know this fact because of an inventory compiled in 1819 and 1820 of the house and its furnishings.

The house remained in the Myers family until 1930, when it was acquired, through the efforts of Mrs. Fergus Reid, by a public-spirited group of citizens known as the Colonial House Corporations. They opened the house to the public and twenty years later presented it to the City of Norfolk. At that time, it was placed in the custody of the Norfolk Museum of Arts and Sciences. In 1961, following an extensive restoration of the house and gardens by Architect Finlay F. Ferguson, Jr., the Myers House was reopened to the public. The stable, coach house, wash house, necessary (privy), and well are still to be restored.

Moses Myers died July 8, 1835, but his history can never be forgotten as long as this beautiful dwelling and its furnishing remain intact for all to see. Today, the halls and the rooms echo with the footsteps of tourists who come to learn the story of the early American family who were the first Jewish citizens of Norfolk, Virginia, and of their contributions to their community and to their country.

The Richmond Jewish Community

The Importance of Religious Freedom

Jacob I. Cohen. He and his partner, Isaiah Isaacs, had a store called "The Jew's Store," and hired Daniel Boone to do land surveys for them.

AMONG the Jewish communities in early America, Richmond, Virginia was very late. The first American Jewish communities had been established in New York in 1654, followed by communities in Philadelphia, Newport, Charleston, and Savannah. It wasn't until 1789 that Richmond had a Jewish population that could be called a community.

Why did it take so long for Jews to gather in Richmond? After all, Virginia had been the home of the earliest established English-American colony, Jamestown in 1607. It was also the most populated of the original thirteen colonies. It was a fertile area, in terms of both its soil and its economic resources. Why, then, was it the last of the major early American Jewish communities to form?

There were two primary reasons. First, the original colony of Virginia was primarily rural, made up of individual landed estates. There were no large cities along waterways so necessary for trade and commerce and mercantilism. Since most of the Jews in early America were part of the merchant class, they developed their communities in other places, in ports where ships came and went, carrying cargo from England, Europe, and other countries around the world.

The second reason involved the Jewish requirement for religious tolerance. The government of colonial Virginia was strongly tied to the Anglican Christian Church of England. No one could become a citizen of Virginia unless he or she took an oath of faith to the Christian church and to Jesus Christ. Since

Jews did not swear allegiance to Jesus Christ, they were not welcome. They could not own land, practice their religion openly without fear of malice, vote, or have a voice in the affairs of government. This was the case until Virginia's church-and-state relationship was challenged by one of that state's most prominent landowners, philosophers, and politicians, Thomas Jefferson.

Thomas Jefferson, strongly influenced by the sixteenth-century English philosopher John Locke, was an outspoken and eloquent proponent of liberty, human rights, and religious tolerance. He believed that freedom of the intellect was necessary for the growth of a democratic society. To promote that freedom and to promote democracy, he called for a separation between church and state, so that complete religious freedom might thrive.

These views inspired the Declaration of Independence, which Jefferson helped to write in 1776. Shortly thereafter, he wrote the "Virginia Statute for Religious Freedom in Virginia." Based on the principles and writings of John Locke and on passages in the Old Testament, Jefferson's bill called for the complete separation of church and state in Virginia and equal rights for "the Jew and the Gentile, the Christian and the Mohamentan, the Hindu, the infidel...." (This description is from Jefferson's autobiography, not from the statute itself.)

Jefferson's bill was not accepted immediately. It was initially defeated, and it was not enacted until 1786. But the guarantee that it provided was worth the wait, because it extended the principle of liberty to Jews with the promise "of no civil detriment for their beliefs" in the state of Virginia. The bill was a charter of religious liberty for Jews in America, and it served as an example for other states as well. In 1791, the First Amendment to the United States Constitution guaranteed religious freedom and the separation of church and state.

Jews were quick to respond to the new religious tolerance to be found in Virginia, which brought civil rights and economic benefits as well. A small group of Jewish citizens came to form a community in Richmond. Starting with four families, their numbers grew quickly. By 1789, there was a minyan of ten men, and they began to build the first congregation in Richmond, known as Kahal Kodosh Beth Shalome, House of Peace. By 1790, the newly formed community served twenty Jewish families, or approximately a hundred people. Jews also began playing an important part in the history of the city, a relationship that continues to this day involving the areas of economics, social service, and multicultural exchanges of ideas.

*   *   *

No. III.

An ACT *for eſtabliſhing* RELIGIOUS FREEDOM, *paſſed in the Aſſembly of Virginia in the beginning of the year* 1786.

WELL aware that Almighty God hath created the mind free ; that all attempts to influence it by temporal puniſhments or burdens, or by civil incapacitations, tend only to beget habits of hypocrify and meanneſs, and are a departure from the plan of the Holy Author of our religion, who being Lord both of body and mind, yet choſe not to propagate it by coercions on either, as was in his Almighty power to do ; that the impious preſumption of legiſlators and rulers, civil as well as eccleſiaſtical, who, being themſelves but fallible and uninſpired men have aſſumed dominion over the faith of others, ſetting up their own opinions and modes of thinking as the only true and infallible, and as ſuch endeavouring to impoſe them on others, hath eſtabliſhed and maintained falſe religions over the greateſt part of the world, and through all time ; that to compel a man to furniſh contributions

of

"Act for establishing religious freedom" in Virginia. These words, written by Thomas Jefferson, gave Catholics, Jews, Moslems, heathens, and atheists the right to live freely as their consciences dictated. Only after this act was written did a Jewish community become established in Virginia.

The important Jewish citizens in the rapidly growing community of Richmond, Virginia, included Jacob I. Cohen, one of the founders of Beth Shalome. Jacob I. Cohen was born on January 2, 1744, in Oberdorf, Germany, the son of Joshua and Peschal Cohen. Coming by way of England, Jacob immigrated to America in 1773. He lived for a short time in Lancaster, Pennsylvania, and then moved to Charleston, South Carolina, where he enlisted in Captain Lushington's Company, which was part of the Charleston Regiment of Militia during the Revolutionary War. In 1779, Cohen participated in the defense of Charleston against the British. He was hailed by Captain Lushington after the war as a man of much respect, good soldiering, and a man of great courage.

In 1782, in Philadelphia, Jacob I. Cohen asked to become a member of Congregation Mikveh Israel and permission to marry Esther Mordecai, a widow and a former Christian who had embraced Judaism prior to her marriage to Mordecai. According to rabbinic law, a Cohen, of priestly origin, could not marry either a proselyte or a divorcee. Permission was not granted by the Bet Din, the local authority of Jewish law. Cohen defiantly married Esther Mordecai a few days later, and narrowly escaped the only threat of excommunication by Mikveh Israel. It is not known who performed the ceremony.

By 1783 or 1784, Jacob Cohen had moved to Richmond, Virginia. There he went into a successful business with the first Jew to reside in Richmond, Isaiah Isaacs, a silversmith. Their relationship was to last until 1792. Early in their relationship, both Cohen and Isaacs became naturalized American citizens. The firm of Cohen & Isaacs was involved in land speculation and mercantile ventures, and it also operated the first tavern in Richmond. They also dealt in silver, tobacco, sugar, flour, and frying pans. The retail part of this venture was famous throughout Virginia as "The Jew's Store." Their business license (an original copy of which is in the United States National Archives in Washington, D.C.) was officially issued in Hebrew.

In conjunction with their store, the partners also owned numerous real estate holdings. As a result, they got involved with land speculation and development, not only in Virginia, but in the bordering Kentucky and Ohio frontiers as well. Often the land had to be surveyed, and in 1781, Cohen and Isaacs hired a young frontiersman named Daniel Boone to survey ten thousand acres of land in the neighboring Licking River area of Kentucky. A copy of Boone's surveying receipt is housed in the United States Library of Congress. Cohen and Isaacs also owned a lead mine in Powhatan, Kentucky. Customers their business serviced included James Madison, before he became President, and Edmond Randolf, who signed the Declaration of Independence.

Both Cohen and Isaacs were founders of the first synagogue in Richmond,

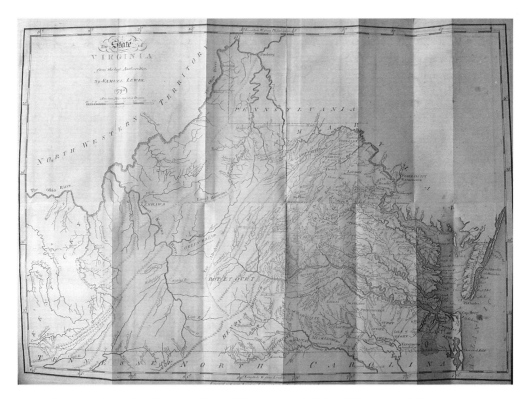

Map of Virginia drawn by Thomas Jefferson. The map is included in Jefferson's book Notes on the State of Virginia, *as is the act establishing religious freedom quoted on page 137.*

Beth Shalome, founded in 1789. Cohen was also a Mason and a member of Richmond's Common Hall, the predecessor of Richmond's Chamber of Commerce, and a Trustee of the Richmond Jewish Cemetery. He was also appointed to the board of inspectors of the State Penitentiary in 1807 by the Governor of Virginia, James Monroe.

Richmond, at that time, was mostly a rural community, still entrenched in the Southern way of life; therefore, the Cohen–Isaacs businesses owned several slaves. Early in the 1790's, however, Cohen and Isaacs freed their slaves, giving them each twenty-five dollars. Cohen strongly believed in human personal rights, having benefited from Jefferson's philosophy of tolerance, and by extending that philosophy to freeing his slaves, he hoped he could influence others in his community as well.

Jacob Cohen's portrait, attributed to Charles Wilson Peale, was painted around 1800, when Cohen was fifty-six years of age. Cohen is shown with dark eyes and gray hair. He's wearing a black coat, a white waistcoat, stockings, and a jabot (ruffles on the front of a shirt). He is seated on a chair with a red coverlet, and the background of the painting is reddish brown. The painting is unsigned.

Jacob Cohen's patriotism was exhibited not only in his Revolutionary War service, but also in the commitments he expressed to the new republic in a document called "A Prayer for the Country." This treatise was delivered on Thanksgiving in 1789 to celebrate the acceptance of the United States Constitution, and the prayer, when written out, cleverly contains George Washington's name in a Hebrew acrostic. Washington had been inaugurated in April of the same year.

When he died, Jacob I. Cohen's last will and testament established a library in Richmond, to be watched over by his nephew, Joshua, which contained volumes dealing with Jewish subjects, as well as books on art, philosophy, music, and literature.

Solomon Jacobs came to Richmond from Philadelphia. Compared to Philadelphia, which he said was "full of conspicuous consumption," he found Richmond dull and the people unrefined, but he said they were more honest and ten times as hospitable as those in the Philadelphia community. In Richmond he established himself as a successful tobacco merchant. He was known as an outspoken eccentric, but that did not interfere with a highly successful career. He was Director of the Farmer's Bank of Virginia. In 1813, he was also elected to the Common Hall or City Council, where he subsequently served as Alderman and Recorder and at one point was appointed Acting Mayor. He was a Grand Master of the Masonic Lodge in Virginia from 1810 to 1813. He was also President of Beth Shalome. In 1815, he married Hetty Nones, daughter of the Revolutionary War hero, Benjamin Nones of Philadelphia.

Perry De Leon, of Richmond, Virginia, a great-grandson of Solomon Jacobs, wrote that he owned a portrait in oil of his great-grandfather. He described Jacobs as wearing a "claret colored coat with gilt buttons, a ruffled shirt or jabot." He said that his grandfather had delicate and refined features, powdered gray hair, and brown eyes. He was posed in front of a bluish-gray background. Today, that portrait is housed at the Pennsylvania Academy of Fine Arts in Philadelphia.

The Reverend Isaac B. Seixas came to Richmond in 1792, to serve as the religious leader of Beth Shalome Congregation. He was a nephew of the Reverend Gershom Seixas, who had served New York's Congregation Shearith Israel for forty years. Isaac Seixas helped to build the 1820 Beth Shalome edifice, noting that it looked just like a Virginia church. Seixas taught Hebrew and German to his congregation and Hebrew to George Wythe, a prominent citizen and lawyer of Williamsburg, Virginia. Seixas continued to serve his congregation in this capacity until 1828, when he moved to New York.

Another one of the Jewish students that Isaac Seixas taught was Isaac Leeser, who founded the Anglo-Jewish monthly newspaper in Philadelphia called *The Occident*. Leeser himself became a prolific author and translator of the Bible, and in 1829 his articles in defense of Jews were published in the Richmond newspaper.

In 1790, Congregation Beth Shalome organized its first cemetery land. At that time it also formed a group called the Ezrach Ochim, a society for the relief of indigent travelers, setting an example for other Jewish communities in America to follow. The society offered help to visitors for three days and three nights, and longer if needed, subject to the approval of the majority of the participating directors.

One of the travelers helped in the early years of the society's formation was Hyam Samuels from Hamburg, Germany. He settled first in Richmond and then in Petersburg, thirty miles away. He advertised "Timepieces in clocks as accurate as the finest products anywhere." Hyam's wife, Rebecca was not happy in Petersburg, and her letters home to her parents in Europe show that she resented the lack of Jewish observance by her Jewish neighbors in The Old Dominion, as Virginia was called then, noting, for example, that Jews in Virginia kept shops open on Saturdays.

Colonial America suffered a high rate of infant mortality. About forty percent of all children died in infancy; only the heartiest survived. This new and rugged land was hard on women too, for many a mother died in childbirth and left her bereft husband with a family of children to raise. One of these widowed fathers was Jacob Mordecai, a shopkeeper in the North Carolina village of Warrenton. When Judith Myers, his wife, died, she left him with six children. Because he could not raise all of them himself, he sent two of his daughters to live with his kinfolk in Richmond. He kept in touch with his daughters, Rachel and Ellen, who were then eight and seven years of age, by writing them and telling them how to behave. By our standards, most of his letters to the children were pedantic and stodgy. He always addressed them as if they were mature women, not little children. In one letter, however, he wrote like a father and a warm human being, even by modern standards.

My dear Rachel and Ellen:

Be good girls, mind your reading and writing, that you may be able to send me letters often, for I love you so dearly that I shall always be pleased when you can write to me. God bless you, my dear children. Love each other and mind your dear uncles and then you will always afford pleasure to your papa.

I participate with you at this remote distance in the pleasure that will attend the recet [receipt] of these few lines which will be delivered by your beloved brother Moses. He will give you all the news and every information respecting your brothers, who are in health and both send an abundance of love to you. Solly says he is going to Petersburg next week to see his sisters and has several horses in readiness.

I hope my dear Rachel has received the book I sent to the care of Uncle Samson some time past. The bearer has another in charge from me, with some other trifles which you will accept as a mark of my love for you, my dear girls. Tell Ellen my lops have not diminished in consequence of the kisses she gave me, and that I long to press her to my heart.

Your affectionate father, J.M.

There is a brass seal and traveling inkwell still in Richmond that belonged to Jacob Mordecai. After a decade of teaching Mordecai returned to Richmond and to his two daughters. There he served as Parnass or President of Beth Shalome Synagogue, and there he lived out his years.

Of all of the families connected with the early Jewish community in Richmond, the Myers family, large in number and scope, remains the most prominent in Virginia history.

The Myers family of Richmond started with two sons of the famed New York silversmith Myer Myers. In 1796, Samuel Myers and his half brother, Moses Mears Myers, married two sisters, Judith and Sally Hays, the daughters of Moses Michael Hays, a founder of the Bank of Boston, Massachusetts. Moses Michael Hays had wedding gifts made for them by another important Colonial silversmith, Paul Revere. He also had a marriage contract or prenuptial agreement drawn up for his daughter, Judith, when she married Samuel. The Hays family was very wealthy, and it was important to him to protect his children's future inheritance.

It was about this time that the two young couples moved to Richmond, and by 1800 Samuel Myers had established himself as a leading citizen. Both

Exterior of Congregation Beth Shalome, Richmond. The building is in the Georgian style, with a fan light window over the front door and shuttered arched windows on either side of the brick facade.

Samuel and Moses performed a vital function for the colonies. As merchants, they dealt in wheat, tobacco, cotton, and luxury items like French brandy as well as much needed ammunition. Samuel was appointed to the Board of Aldermen, and in 1817 he became Director of the United States Bank. Samuel Myers appears in the 1819 Richmond directory as a merchant, his place of business on Fourteenth Street.

Samuel's home was near the synagogue, Beth Shalome. It was a large brick house with a garden that occupied three quarters of a block. The interior of his home, he proudly noted in his diary, was known for its carved and white painted woodwork and gray marble fireplaces with graceful fluted columns. Arched and recessed bookshelves were on either side of the fireplace in the drawing room.

In the records of Mrs. Edward (Caroline) Cohen, privately printed in 1913, Samuel was thus described: "His cold and dignified demeanor created an impression of severity which has become a tradition among his descendants.

Judith Hays Myers, wife of Samuel Myers. Her wedding gifts included a silver teapot made by Paul Revere on order from her father, Moses Michael Hays.

In appearance, he was handsome, very refined and elegant looking." He had a strong chin and glowing eyes. Samuel's dignified demeanor can be seen in the portrait painted by Gilbert Stuart in 1816.

Samuel and Judith were close friends of a young lawyer in Virginia named John Marshall, who would eventually become Chief Justice of the United States Supreme Court.

Samuel and Judith had six children. One of them, a son named Gustavus Adolphus Myers, born in 1801, was described by a contemporary as a "fine lawyer, patron of the arts, very witty and charming, an ornament to Richmond Society, to the Richmond Bar Association, and greatly beloved." In addition to being a respected lawyer, Myers also served on the founding board of the Virginia Historical Society, which supplied some of the information necessary to write this chapter. His portrait is prominently hung on the walls of the Society in Richmond.

*   *   *

Samuel Myers. This son of the famed New York silversmith Myer Myers was a merchant. He was active at Beth Shalome Congregation when he married Judith Hays after agreeing to a marriage contract drawn up by her father, Moses Michael Hays.

Another important citizen of Richmond was Joseph Marx, who was considered the most affluent member of the Richmond Jewish community in the early nineteenth century. He was a merchant who traded with Holland, Germany, and England, dealing in sugar, iron, gunpowder, tobacco, and fine flour. He lived in an elegant house with pillars, and he was known to have a fine library. He was an intellectual as well as a merchant, and he corresponded with Thomas Jefferson on issues of commerce and on literary matters.

The Jews in Richmond honored the Jewish traditions, but like the Jews of the other early Jewish-American communities, they also became involved in the general and secular aspects of community life. In politics, religion, social reform, education, and the arts, Jews in Richmond responded to the needs of life around them. The rabbis of Beth Shalome reached out to the community, to promote better understanding between faiths in a state and a nation that had officially adopted the philosophy of religious tolerance. And those hardy men and women who founded Beth Shalome were an integral part, not just of the building of Richmond, but of the development of the new United States as well. Their valuable contributions have not been forgotten.

The experience of Virginia's Jewish population illustrates the principles set forth by Thomas Jefferson—that freedom of the intellect is necessary for the growth of a democratic society.

Four Early American Women

History Revealed
Through Women's Words

Grace Seixas Nathan, wife of Simon Nathan and sister of Reverend Gershom Mendes Seixas. Born in New York in 1752 and educated only to the grammar school level, Grace Seixas Nathan was nonetheless able to communicate her feelings through her poems. She wrote about her pain at the loss of her grandchildren, and also about her own sense of patriotism.

WOMEN of the colonial period and the early years of the republic have largely been overlooked by history and have remained in the shadow of their often heralded and honored husbands. Those women who are remembered today are often thought about for reasons outside their own achievements. Martha Washington, for example, is primarily known as her husband's wife; and even Betsy Ross, who crafted the first American flag, is considered part of the George Washington story. The story of colonial and early America is, for the most part, the study of important men.

There were, however, many women in that period who had thought-provoking minds, and it is important that we pay attention to what they had to say. These outspoken and often opinionated women provide a different look at the history of early America, and we may read their words which have been preserved in the letters, poetry, and prose that they wrote to family and friends.

Here are four such women. They were strong-minded and inquisitive. They were American and they were also Jewish. Reading their words reveals their strengths, their talents, and their achievements.

The first is Grace Seixas Nathan. Grace was born in 1752. She was the wife of Simon Nathan, a Revolutionary War merchant. She was also the sister of the famed New York rabbi, Gershom Mendes Seixas. Her education was probably limited to the elementary schooling given the girls of her pre-Revolutionary generation. Nonetheless, Grace developed literary interests and she eventually wrote down her feelings in letters, poems, and what she called "ethical thoughts." Like her brother, Gershom, she was a pious and devoted Jew. In 1782, while residing in Philadelphia, she and Rebecca Machado Phillips donated the cloth for the Tebah for the reader's desk and curtains for the ark of the new Philadelphia synagogue, Mikveh Israel.

Grace was also ardently public-spirited. During the War of 1812, she wrote in one of her "ethical thoughts," "I cannot for the life of me feel terrified. Besides, I am so true an American, so warm a patriot that I hold these mighty armies and their proud, arrogant, presumptuous and overpowering nation [Great Britain] as beings that we have conquered and shall conquer again." Her words are strong, vigorous, and well articulated. She was obviously clear in her loyalties.

In 1819, when one of her grandchildren died, Grace expressed her grief in this elegant poem:

> I had a bud so very sweet—its fragrance reached the skies.
> The angels joined in holy league—and seized it as their prize.
> They bore it to their realms of bliss—where it will ever bloom,
> For in the bosom of their God they place my rich perfume.

This poem reveals not only her grief at her time of deep mourning, but her loving feelings for the child, whom she likened to the perfume placed in the bosom of God. This metaphor illustrates the custom of those times, when people did not bathe as often or as regularly as they do today. In order to smell as sweet as possible, a woman would place in her bodice, right next to her bosom, a *tussie mussie* made of fragrant flowers, such as roses, along with fragrant herbs, such as lavender or lemon balm.

Because many early American Jewish women were married to merchants who traveled extensively, they often endured long periods of separation and loneliness, which might last for months or even years while their husbands were away on the frontier, or in other colonies, or abroad. These wives learned to live with fears of Indian attacks on their men, or the pirating of their merchant ships, or devastating storms at sea. Fear and loneliness became these women's constant companions.

For example, in 1792, Miriam Gratz of Philadelphia wrote to her well-known and respected husband, Michael, who was away on a business trip, "I thank you, Dear, for your good advice in advising me to be contented and

Miriam Gratz, wife of Michael Gratz. Michael Gratz often had to travel from home in Philadelphia to conduct his business overseas, and in his absence Miriam wrote of her fears for his safety.

happy in your absence. I assure you I shall endeavor to be as much as possible, though you know very well that I have many anxious thoughts about you. I pray the almighty may prosper you in all of your undertakings, conduct you safe over the wide oashan—safe to me and our children."

A letter dated September 5, 1806, reveals the loneliness of Frances Isaacs Hendricks of New York. She was writing to her highly successful husband, Harmon, who worked in the copper manufacturing business which his family helped to bring to the colonies from England.

> I take care the fires put out and the door locked as you requested before I go to bed. Uriah [their son] is, thank god, in perfect health. I can't get him to understand your mode of travel, he does not know what a stage is—asks continuously if you have a horse of your own.
>
> I wish your return and I am sure you will not remain an hour longer than your business requires.

Frances Isaacs Hendricks, wife of Harmon Hendricks. Like other merchants, Harmon Hendricks traveled often, and Frances's letters kept him up to date about their children and her loneliness during his absences from home.

My dearest Harmon, that you may enjoy every possible satisfaction, absent from your Frances, is her sincere wish.

Rebecca Alexander Samuels, who was born in Central Europe, wanted to live as a Jew. She kept the holidays and the Sabbath. She taught her three-year-old daughter to read the Hebrew prayers. Through her letters we know that she was impressed by the spirit of America and she was delighted that in America there were no Hahams who could order her around religiously. This was a fine country!

Unlike Grace Seixas Nathan and Frances Isaacs Hendricks of New York or Miriam Gratz of Philadelphia, all of whom lived in large, organized Jewish communities, Rebecca Samuels lived in Petersburg, Virginia, a small, isolated town about thirty miles from Richmond. She had moved there in 1790, with her husband, a highly skilled maker of watches and clocks.

In the letters she wrote home to her parents in Europe, she addressed many subjects important to Jews living in America, such as anti-Jewish German prejudice, acculturation, the separation of Church and State, observances of craft guild restrictions, and larger opportunities available in the country for the common man. She also noted, unhappily, that Jews in Virginia kept shops open on Saturdays. And she longed to see a synagogue. Rebecca eventually moved from Petersburg when she realized that it was no place to keep traditions alive.

In a letter to her parents back in Poland, which she wrote in 1791, she reveals much about the immigrant Jewish experience of that era:

Dear Parents,

I know quite well you will not want me to bring up my children like Gentiles. Here they cannot become anything else. Jewishness is pushed aside here. There are here [in Petersburg] ten or twelve Jews, and they are not worthy of being called Jews. We have a shochet here who goes to market and buys trefah [nonkosher] meat and then brings it home. On Rosh Hashanah and on Yom Kippur the people worshipped here without one sefer torah and not one of them wore the tallit or abra kanfot [the small fringes worn on the body], except Hyman and my Sammy's godfather. The latter is an old man of sixty, a man from Holland. He has been in America for thirty years already, for twenty years he was in Charleston, and he has been living here for four years. He does not want to remain here any longer and will go with us to Charleston. In that place there is a blessed community of three hundred Jews.

You can believe me that I crave to see a synagogue to which I can go. The way we live now is no life at all. We do not know what the Sabbath and holidays are. On the Sabbath all the Jewish shops are open, and they do business on that day as they do throughout the week. But ours we do not allow to open. With us there is still some Sabbath. You must believe me that in our house we all live as Jews as much as we can.

All the people who hear that we are leaving give us their blessings. They say that it is sinful that such blessed children should be brought up here in Petersburg. My children cannot learn anything here, nothing Jewish, nothing of general culture. My Schoene [my daughter], God bless her, is already three years old, I think it is time that she should learn something, and she has a good head to learn. I have taught her the bedtime prayers and grace after meals in just two lessons. I believe that no one among the Jews here can do as well as she. And my Sammy [born in 1790], God bless him is already beginning to talk.

I could write more. However, I do not have any more paper.

Paper was an important commodity for Rebecca Samuels, as it also was for Miriam Gratz, Frances Isaacs Hendricks, and Grace Seixas Nathan. Their inquisitive and thought-provoking writings reveal that they cherished the right to relate their own feelings and thoughts about important matters both personal and general. We are fortunate that these four women—and many others like them—chose to write down their thoughts and give us the perspective we need to understand the history of the Jews in early America.

What strong characters they must have had, these outspoken and often opinionated early American Jewish women. Remembered and known for their own achievements, none of them can be accused of living in the shadow of their husbands. Rather, each lives in her own prominence.

Mordecai Manuel Noah

*Diplomat, Writer,
and Political Philosopher*

*Mordecai Manuel Noah, from the frontispiece of
his book,* Travels in England, France, Spain,
and the Barbary States.

B ORN in Philadelphia in 1785, Mordecai Manuel Noah exemplified Jewish
participation in both the movement towards American Zionism and the integration of Jews into the activities of life in
America at the national level. Noah came
from a family that had had direct involve-
ment in the creation of the United States
laws. His grandfather was Jonas Phillips, a
Revolutionary War hero from Philadelphia
and a signer of the Non-Importation Agreement, which said to England there
could be no taxation without representation during the pre-Revolutionary
Colonial War era in America.

Because Mordecai's mother died early in Mordecai's life, the boy was
raised by his grandfather, Jonas, and thus he became exposed to and involved
in his grandfather's political philosophy and actions. He was aware that his
grandfather had written a letter to the Federal Constitutional Convention in
Philadelphia, asking that equal rights be granted to all men, including the
right to take part politically in all of American life. Jonas asked for this because
the constitution of his own state, Pennsylvania, did not grant these rights to all
men.

With this kind of background, it is easy to see where Noah's enthusiasm for
participation in his country's affairs came from. At the age of twenty-three,
Noah had already been writing creatively for ten years, and had just finished
his first play, *The Fortress of Sorrento.* The subject of this play was the libertari-

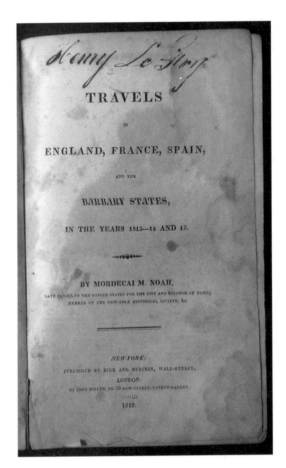

Travels in England, France, Spain, and the Barbary States... *by Mordecai Manuel Noah. The book was printed in 1819, after Noah returned from Tunisia, where Noah served as America's first Jewish ambassador. Noah shared the liberal views of Thomas Jefferson and supported the Democratic ways of his grandfather, Jonas Phillips.*

an views of Thomas Jefferson, and it showed Noah's pride in being associated with the political Democrats of his generation. In his writing, Noah expressed his great faith in humanity and the power of the human spirit.

Mordecai Manuel Noah was still in his twenties when he became the first Jew to fill a high diplomatic post in the Foreign Service. He was appointed Consul to Tunis by President James Madison during the war of 1812.

In 1817, Noah was the editor of a paper called *National Advocate.* In time he would also be a part of five other publications, including the *Philadelphia Inquirer* and the *Sunday Times,* all of which he either started or edited. Writing for all of these papers, he always stressed and was dedicated to Jeffersonian principles of natural and inalienable rights for all men.

Through all of this time, Noah was a faithful member of Congregation Shearith Israel in New York.

In 1817, Noah was the chief orator at the forty-first anniversary celebration of America's Independence in the state of New York. He emphasized his belief that the discussion of national affairs, including political differences, was an important and healthy exercise in which all people in the United States should participate. Recognized by President James Madison for these thoughts, Mordecai agreed that healthy discussions could produce healthy changes in all areas of national life.

In New York in 1819, Noah wrote his famous *Travels in England, France, Spain and the Barbary States in the Years 1813–14 and 15*. This discussion was published by Kirk and Mercier under the auspices of the New York Historical Society and was disseminated widely throughout New York and the other states. It was written because Noah wanted to explain the legitimacy of his appointment in Tunisia and importance of the work he had accomplished for the United States at that time, working toward a goal of better and more positive world relations. He did this in response to some of his political enemies' allegations that he had used the appointment in Tunisia for his own gain. He flatly denied any such reasons.

In 1828, Noah was appointed the High Sheriff in New York. In this role, he publicly spoke out against acts of violence, including the assault on himself by one Elijah Roberts.

Of all his many accomplishments, Noah is perhaps best known for his utopian dream of founding a Jewish colony in 1825 named Ararat, on Grand Island in the Niagara River, near Buffalo, New York. Ararat was to be a safe haven for Jews. This dream never became a reality; it was a vision ahead of its time. Noah also proposed that America help purchase Palestine from Turkey to establish a safe home for the oppressed Jews of Europe. This visionary proposal was made many years before the political movement with the same goal, called Zionism.

During his lifetime, Noah communicated with three United States presidents: John Adams, James Madison, and Thomas Jefferson. These interchanges involved discussions of the human condition, the nation's laws, and liberty for all. He always said there was much still to be done. He adamantly expressed controversial views all his life. For example, Noah considered the Native American Indians to be descended from the Lost Tribes of Israel. For this reason, these people deserved to be treated far better than they were by the citizens and government of this American nation. The American Indians, in

Mordecai Manuel Noah in middle age. Noah was a prolific writer, not only of political papers and opinions, but also of plays, the first of which was The Fortress of Sorrento.

Noah's opinion, deserved the same rights as all other citizens received.

Mordecai Manuel Noah's portrait is an oil on canvas painted by the well-known American artist, John Wesley Jarvis. From this portrait, we can see that he was physically rotund, a man of large frame, portly and balding, but posed to show that he was a very important gentleman.

In 1851, Noah died. Known as a faithful Jew through and through, he was said to have a kind heart and generous sympathies towards all forms of Judaism. He is remembered as a journalist, a politician, a playwright, and a statesman, but mostly as an ardent and dedicated spokesman for human rights.

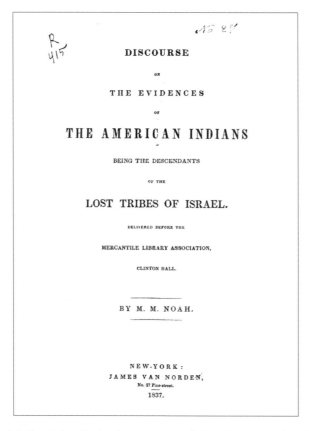

Mordecai Noah believed that Native Americans revealed in their rituals that they might be part of the Lost Tribes of Israel. Radical in his thinking, he also proposed the Island of Ararat, near Buffalo, New York, as a haven for Jews.

Uriah
Phillips Levy

He Saved Monticello

URIAH Phillips Levy was born in 1792 in Philadelphia, the son of Michael Levy and Rachel Phillips Levy. His ancestors on his mother's side are traceable all the way back to the fifteenth century in Spain, and they include many advisors to kings and queens who ruled in the Iberian Peninsula. Uriah was also the grandson of Jonas Phillips, the much-honored soldier who had served in the Revolutionary War. Jonas Phillips was also an important historical figure because of his letter to the Constitu-

Uriah Phillips Levy. After going to sea from age ten to age twelve, he returned to Philadelphia to study for his Bar Mitzvah at Congregation Mikveh Israel. He went to sea again at age fourteen, eventually to become a commodore, the first Jew to do so in the American Navy.

tional Convention in 1787, in which he protested the possible inclusion of an oath of belief in the divine inspiration of the New Testament. As we shall see, Uriah Levy shared his grandfather's passion for religious freedom as a necessary ingredient of democracy. Jonas had also served as the Parnass or President of Congregation Mikveh Israel in Philadelphia, and had also been the congregation's shochet, or ritual slaughterer. Uriah, growing up, faithfully attended the same congregation as his grandfather, where he received his early religious training.

Philadelphia, at that time, was one of America's most important shipping ports, located on the Delaware River, which leads directly into the Atlantic Ocean. Uriah fell in love with the sea early, and at the age of ten, despite his parents' objections, he joined the crew of a vessel called *The New Jerusalem* and shipped out to sea as a cabin boy. He remained on the ship for two years, at the end of which time he came home to prepare for his Bar Mitzvah.

He studied for his Bar Mitzvah with Amos Hart, a learned Jew who had recently arrived from Holland. Hart was also a ship's furnisher, by trade, and knew a great deal about the sea. Young Levy managed to acquire as much knowledge of winds and waves as he did of Torah. In any case, on the Shabbat following his thirteenth birthday, Uriah was called to the Torah for the reading of his portion. After the service, his parents gave a feast in their son's honor and Uriah delivered an appropriate address to his guests.

During the next year, Uriah was very involved in the synagogue's activities, but shortly after his fourteenth birthday, Uriah went to sea again, this time as a common seaman on a merchant ship. Although his parents tried again to discourage this decision, they finally gave in to his wishes and offered their blessings.

Uriah was twenty years old in 1812, the year of what has been called the second American war for independence. The War of 1812 was largely a naval war, and in fact was fought over the issue of the right of American vessels to sail the legal seas unmolested. It was in this war that Levy, the patriot, decided to make the United States Navy his career.

However, the Navy wasn't an easy place for any Jew. Uriah adhered to his Jewish beliefs; he refused to eat pork or shellfish, and he didn't mix milk and meat together because of the laws of Kashrut. Because of these dietary practices, and because he was open about his Judaism, he was often subjected to vicious acts of anti-Semitism. Often he was flogged, beaten, and whipped. And yet he loved the sea, and was determined to be a part of it. And he refused to give up his religious principles, even though many of his fellow sailors and even the navy itself considered him an undesirable Israelite. He was frequently falsely accused and was court martialed on six different occasions, each time having to appeal the verdict and each time successfully having the unfair decision overturned. Two of the decisions were reversed by presidents James Madison and James Monroe.

Uriah Levy endured anti-Semitic persecution in the navy for the next forty years. Nevertheless, he managed to rise to the high rank of commodore. In this capacity, Levy proved a compassionate officer, always interested in the needs of those under his command. Because of his humanity to his fellow man, his enemies in the Naval Service claimed that he was unfit to be an officer. He was, they said, too soft, not strict enough to be effective in his high military position. They reviled him for refusing to use the cat-o'-nine-tails in disciplining the men under his command. "The cat" was a whip consisting of nine knotted ropes tied together, and was used on the bare backs of sailors who were being disciplined by a naval officer. Uriah insisted that this form of punishment was degrading to the individual and that flogging was associated with slavery.

On one occasion in 1816, Lieutenant William Potter, a big red-faced man and a violent anti-Semite, called Levy a "Dammed Jew." Levy ignored him, but later that evening, Potter pushed Levy, and insulted him three times, finally provoking him into a duel. Before the duel, the judge asked, "Have either of you anything to say?" Uriah replied, "Yes, I want to say a Hebrew prayer." He then recited the Shema. He then added, "I also wish to state that although I am a crack shot, I shall not fire at my opponent and I think it wise if this ridiculous affair be abandoned." Potter insisted that the duel continue. He fired four times at Uriah, who did not lift his pistol. On the fourth shot, he nicked Levy's left ear. Potter then insisted on a fifth round. Finally, Levy lifted his pistol, intending to shoot Potter in the leg. Unfortunately (for Potter), the ball struck Potter in the chest and he fell back dead. There was a naval investigation into the facts surrounding the duel and its results. Levy was cleared of all fault in Potter's demise, for it was clear that he had tried to preserve his opponent's dignity, he had not wanted to fire, and he had not tried to kill him.

The issue of flogging and inhumane discipline became an important part of Uriah Levy's naval career. He knew that it was not at all unusual for a midshipman to receive as many as 250 blows or lashes, and that the punishment was stopped only when a sailor was found by the ship's surgeon to be unfit to receive any more. Moreover, even with a ship's surgeon on board, discipline was generally abused. And so Uriah campaigned passionately and relentlessly to have an anti-flogging clause added to the navy's rules. Finally, in 1850, as a rider to a naval appropriation bill, an anti-flogging bill was added. In July, 1862, Congress outlawed flogging entirely.

With this law, the United States Navy inaugurated new rules for recruiting and training sailors, rules that would make the service more attractive to a better class of seamen. The navy also initiated an apprentice system, which was a more humane type of hierarchy, and its beginnings can be traced to Uriah's passionate efforts to ban flogging once and for all.

During his naval service, Levy commanded the ships, the *Argus,* the *George Washington,* and the frigate *The United States.* It was while he was on *The United States* that he married his cousin, Virginia Lopez, of the famous Sephardic Lopez family of Newport, Rhode Island. In marrying Virginia, he became the first and the only naval officer ever to honeymoon on a naval warship at sea.

At one point in his service, Levy commanded the United States fleet in the Mediterranean. When ordered to bring his fleet home he dispatched one of the ships under his command, *The Macedonia,* to bring back a wagon load of earth from the Holy Land. He presented this earth to his synagogue, the New York congregation, Shearith Israel, for use in traditional Jewish burial services.

Throughout his lifetime, Levy was active in Jewish community affairs. He was the first president of Washington, D.C. Hebrew Congregation and in 1854, he sponsored the new Hebrew School of the B'Nai Jeshuruan Educational Institute in New York.

While on shore in New York, Levy invested in real estate property, and eventually made millions of dollars in the New York real estate market. He must have also gathered many interesting friends along the way. His wife, Virginia, kept a diary and in one entry, for example, she states "Spent Yom Kippur with Baron and Baroness Rothchild of France, who had a synagogue in their home."

Uriah and Virginia never had children, which meant that they had no direct heirs to whom to pass on the great fortune that Uriah had earned in New York. Instead, Uriah devoted much of his fortune during his life and after his death to the cause of preserving Monticello, the home of Thomas Jefferson, to honor the memory of the third President of the United States and to pay respect to the ideals of religious freedom and democracy that Jefferson had championed.

When Thomas Jefferson died on July 4, 1826, he died in debt. He had even had to sell his library in order to keep the roof over his head. He sold those books to the United States government, and they formed the basis for what is now the Library of Congress. After his death, his heirs tried to sell Monticello, the home that Jefferson had designed and built himself. Monticello was considered the manifestation of Jefferson's genius, and the home to his boundless intellect for forty years. It was designed in the classical style of the sixteenth-century architect, Andrea Palladio, with imposing capitals and columns, a style that Jefferson felt would bring him closer to the great minds of antiquity while it also served as a suitable Virginia plantation home. He lived in Monticello for forty years, during which he continually modified it and improved it for the sake of beauty and function.

Nevertheless, after Jefferson's death his heirs were unable to sell the home, and they abandoned the project. Monticello was in danger of abuse and possible destruction. When Uriah Levy heard of this situation, he knew he could not allow the house and gardens of his hero to fall into decay and be lost forever, so he decided to purchase the place in 1834 for the huge sum of $2,700.00. He then spent more money restoring and maintaining the home, where he and Virginia spent their summers. It was his intention to bring Monticello back to its former glory and then to give it to the United States, to honor the man who had drafted the Declaration of Independence, founded the University of Virginia, served as Foreign Minister to France, achieved

Monticello. Thomas Jefferson's home fell into disrepair after his death; Uriah Levy pur-chased it and restored it for all posterity.

greatness as the President of the United States, and had written the Virginia Statute for Religious Freedom.

In his will, Uriah Levy provided for the house and 2,500 adjoining acres to be given either to the United States government or to the state of Virginia. If neither of them wanted it, it was to go to the Hebrew Congregations of New York, Richmond, and Philadelphia. In any case, he wanted to see Monticello preserved for the citizens of the United States to visit, to help them remember all that Thomas Jefferson had done for his country.

Monticello stayed in the Levy family for eighty-nine years, during which they maintained it and gave tours of the estate to the public. Finally, in 1923, the family offered it to the United States government and then to the state of Virginia. Neither party wanted to become responsible for it. At that time a group of proud Virginia citizens formed the non-profit Thomas Jefferson Memorial Foundation, which bought the estate from the Levys.

On the west side of Monticello's grounds today there is a worn granite gravestone that reads, "To the memory of Rachel Phillips Levy, born in New York 23rd of May, 1769, married 1787, died 7 of May, 1839 at Monticello

Gravestone of Rachel Phillips Levy, mother of Commodore Uriah Levy, who died while spending a summer visiting her son at Monticello. The gravestone was recently restored and can be visited today.

Virginia." This stone marks the grave of Uriah's mother, who died on a visit to her son's Virginia home.

Uriah Phillips Levy was a proud man. He stood up for what he believed. At the outbreak of the Civil War, when he was seventy years old, he offered his entire fortune—about three million dollars—to President Lincoln. The President turned down the offer but expressed his gratitude for Levy's patriotism. Expressing that patriotism, Commodore Levy wrote his famous "Memorial to Congress," in which he stated, "I am an American, a sailor, and a Jew."

Today we can see his life-sized portrait, painted by Thomas Sully, which shows a scroll in Levy's hand. The scroll reads, "Author of the abolition of flogging in the United States Navy."

He died in 1862. According to the *New York Herald,* his funeral was remarkable. It combined all the U.S. Naval traditions and honors with a full Jewish funeral service, conducted by Rabbi Lyons of Shearith Israel in New York. Hebrew prayers were recited, and three captains and three lieutenants carried the coffin. They stopped seven times as the Hebrew Psalms were chanted. The Kaddish was recited and dust thrown over his coffin, as is the Jewish burial tradition.

Uriah Phillips Levy has been well remembered for the many contributions

Commodore Levy in later years. Among other accomplishments, Levy is credited with bringing an end to flogging in the navy. He also donated a statue of Thomas Jefferson to the United States government, the first of its kind to be given by a private citizen.

he made to his faith, his country, and his fellow man. During World War I, the destroyer USS *Levy* was named for him. The first permanent Jewish chapel built by the United States Armed Forces is the Commander Levy Chapel at the Norfolk, Virginia Naval Station. At the dedication of the chapel, it was stated, "This ceremony embodies a great tradition—Freedom of religion for the individual and for the community in which he lives." A new chapel is being built today at the United States Naval Academy in Annapolis, Maryland, also to be dedicated to the memory of Commodore Levy. Commodore Levy is now listed in the Jewish-American Hall of Fame, at the Judas Magnus Memorial Museum in Berkeley, California.

These are all appropriate tributes to a man whose life was inspired by passion, pride, and preservation.

Uriah P. Levy Chapel, at the former naval base in Norfolk, Virginia. A new chapel is being built in Levy's name at the U.S. Naval Academy at Annapolis, Maryland.

Isaac Leeser

The First Jewish-American Publisher

Isaac Leeser. A firm believer in Judaic education, beginning with Sunday school for young children, Leeser founded Maimonides College, America's first Jewish theological seminary.

IN ORDER to understand the life and career of Isaac Leeser, an eminent Jewish writer, translator, publisher, and educator, it is important that we know a bit of history of the Jewish community in Philadelphia, Pennsylvania, and especially of the congregation Mikveh Israel.

During the American Revolution, Philadelphia saw a considerable influx of Jews moving to the city. This was because most of the Jews in America were not loyal to the British Crown, and the British at that time were occupying many of the other cities where there were Jewish communities, including New York, Savannah, Newport, and Charleston. When these Jews relocated in Philadelphia, they noticed the cramped quarters of the old house of worship on Elfreth's Alley in the center of Philadelphia. One of these new arrivals was the Reverend Gershom Mendes Seixas, from New York. He and other newcomers decided to help the Philadelphia Jewish community and began to build the first real synagogue structure there, to be known officially as Mikveh Israel. Mordecai Mordecai, a local congregant, received permission from the synagogues in London and Amsterdam to draw and adapt their interior design for the new structure. (The design of this synagogue was in the Portuguese-Spanish style, as were the synagogues in New York and Newport. This reflected the high social status associated with Sephardic society in colonial times, even though most of the Jewish people in the colonies were of Ashkenazic origin. The Sephardic community was considered more

Mikveh Israel Synagogue, interior. Begun in 1771 in rented quarters in Philadelphia, Mikveh Israel became a haven for Jewish New Yorkers fleeing the British during the Revolution. The interior is in typical Sephardic style.

organized, educated, and integrated into society, and hence was considered somewhat of an "aristocracy.")

As often happened in those times, the Philadelphia congregation received financial help from the Jewish communities in other cities—Newport, New York, Curaçao, London, and Amsterdam—and on September 13, 1783, the new shul, Mikveh Israel, was officially opened. By then the importance of the Philadelphia congregation in Jewish America was firmly established.

Isaac Leeser was born in Germany in 1806. At the age of eighteen, he emigrated from the homeland and came to Richmond, Virginia, where he worked for his Uncle Rehine, who taught him about American business. In addition to working for his uncle, young Isaac developed his natural talent for writing. Much of what he wrote concerned the circumstances of the Jews in a primarily Christian society. The Jewish population at that time made up less than one percent of the total population of America.

Mikveh Israel Synagogue, exterior. The red bricks, white shutters, and classical arrangement of windows flanking the door are all typical of the Quaker architectural style, and of many similar buildings in Philadelphia.

In 1829 some of Leeser's articles were published in a Richmond newspaper, and they attracted much attention, not only in Virginia but also as far away as Philadelphia. As a result, Leeser, still only twenty-two years old, was invited to become the Hazzan, or reader, of Mikveh Israel. He moved to Philadelphia and became active in the community there, not only in his position of Hazzan, but also as a writer and as a publisher.

He arrived in Philadelphia with a translation of J. Johlson's *Instruction in the Mosaic Religion*, a catechism used at the prestigious School of Frankfurt am Main. Leeser was surprised to learn that no one in America was willing to take a chance on putting this valuable work into print. He considered the text important for the instruction of young American Israelites of both sexes, who he felt needed more knowledge of their religious roots. There was at that time a great scarcity of elementary textbooks for Jewish children in America.

This marked Isaac Leeser's entry into the field of publishing. In addition to the *Instruction in the Mosaic Religion*, he published in 1838 a Hebrew reader

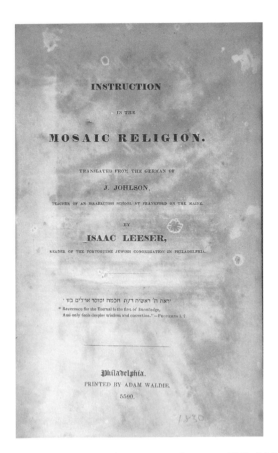

INSTRUCTION

IN THE

MOSAIC RELIGION.

TRANSLATED FROM THE GERMAN OF

J. JOHLSON,

TEACHER OF AN ISRAELITISH SCHOOL AT FRANKFORD ON THE MAINE.

BY

ISAAC LEESER,

READER OF THE PORTUGUESE JEWISH CONGREGATION IN PHILADELPHIA.

יראת ה' ראשית דעת חכמה ומוסר אוילים בזו ׃

" Reverence for the Eternal is the first of knowledge,
And only fools despise wisdom and correction."—Proverbs i. 7.

Philadelphia.
PRINTED BY ADAM WALDIE.
5590.

Isaac Leeser translated Instructions in the Mosaic Religion *in Philadelphia in 1830, while serving as leader of Mikveh Israel Congregation. He was an educator and journalist who wrote about Judaism in America.*

or spelling book in English, and in 1839 a catechism for younger children, also in English. These were important contributions to American Judaic reference resources. All of these works were used at the first congregational Hebrew school in America. Leeser also urged the American Jewish community to form its own rabbinical college, and when his advice was not taken directly, he himself organized the Maimonides Rabbi Training College in Philadelphia. He also translated the Hebrew Bible into English so that the congregation could better understand the message of God.

In addition to the books mentioned, Isaac Leeser also published the first Jewish periodical in the United States, *The Occident and American Jewish Advocate,* beginning in 1843, thus establishing a forum for his outspoken, controversial ideas and those of others. For the next twenty-five years, he became the most prolific American Jewish writer, influencing Jewish communities

The Occident, *vol. 1, no. 1. This newspaper, organized by Isaac Leeser, was one of the first papers dedicated solely to the discussion of Judaism and how it should be practiced in America.*

throughout the United States. Among the titled topics addressed in his publications were "Sunday Laws," "Jewish Children and Gentile Teachers," and "The United States Is Not a Christian State." In *The Occident* he called for the establishing of a competent ecclesiastical authority, schools for religious and general education among all Jews scattered over the Western Hemisphere. In 1867 Isaac Leeser organized the first Jewish school for higher learning in America, the Maimonides College in Philadelphia.

Generally held to be the Father of Conservative Judaism in America, Isaac Leeser was in favor of traditional Jewish worship and outspokenly opposed to the Reform movement, which began in America in 1824, when forty-seven members of the Congregation Beth Elohim in Charleston, South Carolina, petitioned the trustees of the synagogue to drop its original Sephardic service.

Leeser expressed his strong opinion that the Reform movement, originally from Germany, was "undefined, its ground constantly shifting." Furthermore, Leeser said, "No two of them (synagogues) reform on the same principle, endeavoring to uphold every crooked doctrine they propounded by the show of some great authority, uniformly incorrectly quoted." Leeser expressed these explosive opinions in *The Occident,* making it clear that the paper had a mission, and that he, its editor, had strong opinions, an adamant will, and a strong personality.

When Isaac Leeser died in 1868, he had contributed to many aspects of American Jewish culture, as a rabbi, an author, a publisher, a translator, and an educator. In his obituary, it was said that his presence had been interwoven into the whole system of American Judaism.

Solomon Nunes Carvalho

Photographer of the Frontier

Solomon N. Carvalho. A portrait painter and daguerrotypist who painted Abraham Lincoln, Carvalho worked in Charleston, Baltimore, and Philadelphia and was active in the Jewish community.

SOLOMON Nunes Carvalho was a remarkable man, a genius in many ways. He lived from 1815 to 1894, spanning most of the nineteenth century, a time of great exploration—not only of the American continent, but also of technology and philosophy. Carvalho took part in this exploration as a painter, photographer, traveler, scientist, innovator, and philosopher.

The ancestors of the Nunes Carvalho family were associated with the royal court of Portugal, but the family had fled Portugal during the Inquisition, having been labeled Marranos. By the time Solomon was born in 1815, the family was living in Charleston, South Carolina, where his parents were leaders in the Portuguese Israelite Synagogue, Kahal Kodesh Beth Elohim. Solomon's father, David Nunes Carvalho is best known as a leader in the first Reform Movement in America, being instrumental in changing Beth Elohim from a Sephardic service to a reform service in 1824. Young Solomon did not share his father's philosophy of reform Judaism, however, and he remained a devout Orthodox Jew throughout his life.

In 1828, the Carvalho family moved to Baltimore, where they resided on Front Street. There they also had a shop where they made and sold marbled paper to be used in books, either as covers or endsheets. Marbled paper was fashionable elegance in publishing during the seventeenth, eighteenth, and nineteenth centuries, as it is to this day. The family also ran a dry goods store.

In 1834, the family moved again, this time to Philadelphia. Solomon, now nineteen years old, began a career as a professional portrait painter. He showed

Beth Elohim Synagogue, Charleston. The synagogue was designed in the prescribed Sephardic style, with the Torahs at the front of the room and the tevah *or reader's desk in the middle. The synagogue was destroyed by fire in 1838; this picture was drawn from memory by Solomon N. Carvalho. In the nineteenth century, Beth Elohim dropped the Sephardic service and became the first Reform synagogue in America.*

Beth Elohim Synagogue, Charleston. The exteriors of colonial synagogues were designed to blend with the local architecture; Beth Elohim Synagogue was modeled on St. Michael's Church, which still stands in Charleston today.

considerable artistic skill. In fact, when Charleston's Beth Elohim Synagogue burned down, Solomon painted both the inside and the outside of the edifice from memory, so that its renowned beauty would not be forgotten. These paintings remain, serving to illustrate not only Carvalho's talent, but also Charleston's early Jewish history.

In 1845, still in Philadelphia, Solomon married Sara Solis, a member of another well-known Jewish family. They had five children, one of whom, David, became a famous handwriting expert in New York.

In 1849, Solomon and Sara moved back to Baltimore, where he opened an art studio. As he developed as an artist, he experimented with the effects of light and shadow. Influenced by Philadelphia master Thomas Sully, Carvalho painted images that could "float" on the canvas. He used this technique not only for portraits, but also for still lifes and landscapes.

It was during this period that he also became fascinated with the relatively new art form of photography. He experimented with tintypes and with a technique called daguerrotype, developed in France by Louis Jacques Mandé Daguerre and presented to the public in 1839. "Produced directly on a copper surface, daguerrotypes offered an exact representation never before seen. They were small, but their effect on the world was enormous, as they provided an inexpensive and accurate new way of making portraits." Carvalho offered daguerrotype portraits in his art studio, as well as paintings. In fact, he combined the two art forms by hand-coloring the daguerrotype portraits and making them look like paintings.

Solomon Nunes Carvalho's reputation as an artist and photographer grew, and in 1853 he was approached by General John Charles Frémont, an explorer of the American West, who asked Solomon to accompany him as his official photographer on his fifth and last expedition across the frontier to the Pacific Ocean. Frémont wanted Carvalho to record the true facts of his findings and discoveries on the trip, and he planned to put Carvalho's daguerrotype engravings into a book to demonstrate his route through the Rocky Mountains for the forthcoming proposed transcontinental railroad.

This invitation was quite an honor for Carvalho. General Frémont was a well-known and respected explorer, having mapped the Oregon Trail. He had also led expeditions of Forty-Niners to California following the discovery of gold at Sutter's Fort. So Carvalho accepted the invitation and joined the expedition, even though the trip was planned for winter (to show that the route was passable year-round). He had to learn the hard way how to saddle a horse, chop wood, hunt for food, and deal with Native Americans, either by negotiating with them or by protecting himself against their hostile attacks. They traveled through snow and freezing cold, and Carvalho got seriously ill. He would have died, in fact, had a group of Mormons not tended to his recuperation. Through them he met Brigham Young, the leader of the Church of Jesus Christ of Latter-Day Saints and the Governor of the Utah Territory, who became his lifelong friend.

Another problem Carvalho faced was one not shared by his companions: he had to eat forbidden, non-kosher meat in order to survive when the Frémont expedition was forced to slaughter their own animals for food.

The expedition finally reached California, and Solomon Nunes Carvalho decided to stay on there, even after the rest of Frémont's group had returned to the East Coast. He stayed in the settlement of Los Angeles on the Pacific Ocean, where he was helped by the small Jewish community there to find food and shelter. In return for their help, he helped to organize the first Hebrew

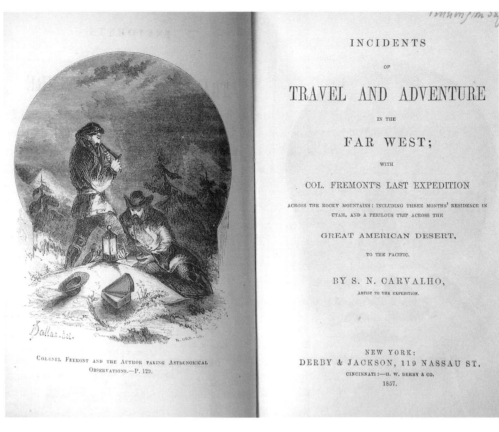

Frontispiece and title page from Solomon N. Carvalho's book describing his adventures as daguerrotypist for Colonel John C. Frémont's fourth and final expedition, which took the company across the Rocky Mountains and the Great Basin deserts to the Pacific Ocean.

Benevolent Society of Los Angeles, patterned after those already functioning in Philadelphia, Charleston, and Baltimore.

Ironically, John Charles Frémont's report of the 1853 expedition was never published, because Frémont lost his journal of the adventure and he also lost all but one of Carvalho's hundred daguerrotypes. By that time Frémont was busy building a political career, as a U.S. senator from the new state of California; he was later to become the first Republican Party candidate for President of the United States. On the other hand, Carvalho's own journal of the trip, which he called *Incidents of Travel and Adventure,* was published. It became the only known record of a survey of the American West during the time Americans were settling into California. Frémont used Carvalho's journal to advance his political career during his unsuccessful presidential campaign.

In his journal, Carvalho stated that the two most rewarding experiences in the adventure through the Rocky Mountains were his first encounter with an American Indian and his first sight of the magnificent American western wilderness. These two revelations demonstrate that Solomon Nunes Carvalho was both a humanist and an artist.

When Carvalho finally returned to Baltimore, he focused all of his creative energy on painting landscapes. In this area of interest, he was influenced by Thomas Cole and Asher Brown Durand, both of whom have become known as members of the Hudson River School, made up of artists who painted landscapes of the beautiful Hudson River Valley in New York State.

At this point in his life, Carvalho began to express his views on religious philosophy. Although he was a devoted Orthodox Jew, he felt that certain changes in Judaism were called for. For example, he felt that the English language should be used more in Jewish prayer books, worship services, and sermons. He published his views in *The Occident,* a Jewish-American monthly paper published in Philadelphia by Isaac Leeser. He also felt that for Judaism to survive in America, Jewish children had to be educated in English as well as Hebrew.

He formed a Portuguese (Sephardic) synagogue in Baltimore; at that time all the other synagogues in Baltimore were of Ashkenazic or German origin. To the opening ceremony of the Lloyd Street Synagogue, Carvalho invited many non-Jews, because he wanted his synagogue to be "a light for Gentiles, that they better understand Jewish traditions."

Solomon's wife, Sara, became the Sunday school teacher, and of course she taught in English. At this school, only women could be officers or teachers, thus making it the first chartered Jewish organization in America to be run entirely by women.

In 1860, Carvalho demonstrated his talent for innovation in yet another way, by inventing an apparatus to improve the efficiency of steam boilers. His invention was eventually used in the U.S. Naval yards in both Baltimore and Washington, D.C. He also wrote a book called *The Two Sciences,* in which he tried to reconcile the theory of evolution with the biblical account of creation, which for an Orthodox traditional Jew was almost unheard of.

Solomon Nunes Carvalho was a man of many talents and accomplishments. He painted the portraits of many important people, including General John Charles Frémont, President Abraham Lincoln, religious leader Brigham Young, Rabbi Judah Touro, and publisher Isaac Leeser. Today his art can be found in many important museums and societies, including the National

Gallery of Art in Washington, D.C., the American Jewish Historical Society in New York, and the Maryland Historical Society in Baltimore.

He was also a pioneer in the field of photography, and an explorer of the American West. He was a humanist, a philosopher, a scientist, and a devout Jew. In his later years, Carvalho was considered a Hebrew scholar and prophet, and was often called upon to comment on various biblical themes and on the poetry of Maimonides, the fifteenth-century Spanish-Jewish scholar.

He remained a colorful figure until his death in 1894. He proved throughout his lifetime that a Jew could participate freely in the culture of American society and still remain loyal to his beloved faith.

Conclusion

Good Taste and Good Deeds

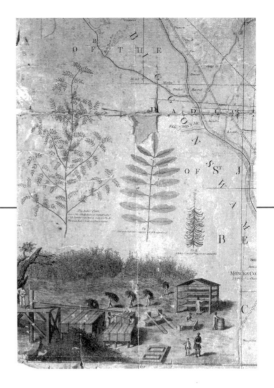

Indigo production in South Carolina. Carolinian indigo was considered even better than that produced in England. Moses Lindo was the Inspector General of Indigo for South Carolina.

THERE is much to be said about the Jewish experience in early America, including the past history of the people who came to settle in this new territory and the causes that led them to venture forth in pursuit of their various dreams.

In America, these new citizens made new and important contributions to the new land. In addition to being dedicated Jews, many of them were ambitious businessmen, inspired artists, excellent scientists, and generous humanitarians. The Jew in early America became involved in what was going on around him, eager to be accepted as a part of society. The more we study the history of this fascinating group of people, the more we understand the importance of their contribution to their new adopted home.

This book has told the stories of a number of important Jewish individuals and families that played a part in the story of early America. These were only a few of the players; of course there were many more. Before closing, I would like to mention a few more examples of Jewish Americans who contributed to society in innovative ways.

For the most part, the Jews in the American colonies belonged to the middle class, and the most important role they played was that of merchants. But Jews played an important role in industry, as well. For example Moses Lindo, who had had much experience with the production of indigo dye in England, brought his trade to Charleston, South Carolina, and helped to establish the

Poem by Penïna Moïse. Penïna was a poet in Charleston, South Carolina, where her family was active at Beth Elohim Sephardic Synagogue. Her poems became hymns when Beth Elohim became the first Reform congregation in America. Penïna was blind, and never married.

production of the dye as both a useful colonial product and a profitable export. It was even thought at one point that the indigo produced at the colonies was a better product than that coming from the mother country. Eventually, Moses Lindo was appointed Surveyor Inspector General of Indigo Dyes and Drugs for the colony. Indigo became a major source of wealth for South Carolina. That Moses Lindo became a man of significant influence is illustrated by a letter he wrote in 1770 to the College of Rhode Island (which later became Brown University) stating that he would not contribute money unless Jewish students were accepted and were not forced to take exams on Saturdays, their Sabbaths.

Charleston was also the home of Penïna Moïse, a poet. She was the daughter of one of the founders of the Sephardic colonial Congregation Beth Elohim in Charleston. The congregation petitioned in 1824 to become the first Reform Synagogue in America, and in 1840, an organ was added to the service to accompany the ritual prayer. Many of Penïna Moïse's poems were made into the hymns used there with the new musical instrument. Many of her hymns are now in the hymnal of the Union of American Hebrew Congregations. She and her sister conducted a school for girls and she served as a leader of the second Jewish Sunday school in America.

By Permission of the Honble *ROBERT DINWIDDIE*, Efq; His Majefty's Lieutenant-Governor, and Commander in Chief of the Colony and Dominion of *Virginia.*

By a Company of Comedians, *from* LONDON, *At the* Theatre *in* Williamsburg, On *Friday* next, being the 15th of *September*, will be prefented, A PLAY, Call'd,

THE
MERCHANT of *VENICE.*

(Written by *Shakefpear.*)
The Part of *ANTONIO* (the Merchant) to be perform'd by

Mr. CLARKSON.

GRATIANO, by Mr. SINGLETON,
Lorenzo, (with Songs in Character) by Mr. ADCOCK.
The Part of *BASSANIO* to be perform'd by

Mr. RIGBY.

Duke, by Mr. Wynell.
Salanio, by Mr. Herbert. *good name*
The Part of *LAUNCELOT,* by Mr. HALLAM.
And the Part of *SHYLOCK,* (the Jew) to be perform'd by

Mr. MALONE.

The Part of *NERISSA,* by Mrs. ADCOCK,
Jeffica, by Mrs. Rigby.
And the Part of *PORTIA,* to be perform'd by

Mrs. HALLAM.

With a new occafional PROLOGUE.
To which will be added, a FARCE, call'd,

The ANATOMIST:
OR,
SHAM DOCTOR.

The Part of *Monfieur le Medecin,* by

Mr. RIGBY.

And the Part of *BEATRICE,* by Mrs. ADCOCK.
⁎⁎⁎ No Perfon, whatfoever, to be admitted behind the Scenes.
BOXES, 7*s.* 6*d.* PIT and BALCONIES, 5*s.* 9*d.* GALLERY, 3*s.* 9*d.*
To begin at Six o'Clock.

Vivat Rex.

Handbill from first American production of Shakespeare's The Merchant of Venice, *at Williamsburg, Virginia. This very anti-Semitic production was also presented in other colonial cities.*

Isaac Harby (1788–1828), known as the leader and founder of the Reformed Society of Israelites, was an outstanding essayist and editor. His "Anniversary Address," delivered before Congregation Beth Elohim November 21, 1825, is today the best known of his literary works. He also wrote the first Reform prayerbook.

In medicine, Dr. D. Nassy, a member of the American Philosophical Society, was the first American Jewish physician to write a medical work, published on November 26, 1793, "Observations on the Cause, Nature, and Treatment of the Epidemic Disorder, Prevalent in Philadelphia."

* * *

Conclusion ———————————————————— 183

COMMEMORATING
FRANCIS SALVADOR
1747 - 1776

FIRST JEW IN SOUTH CAROLINA TO HOLD PUBLIC OFFICE
AND
TO DIE FOR AMERICAN INDEPENDENCE

HE CAME TO CHARLES TOWN FROM HIS NATIVE
LONDON IN 1773 TO DEVELOP EXTENSIVE FAMILY
LANDHOLDINGS IN THE FRONTIER DISTRICT OF
NINETY SIX. AS A DEPUTY TO THE PROVINCIAL
CONGRESSES OF SOUTH CAROLINA, 1775 AND 1776,
HE SERVED WITH DISTINCTION IN THE CREATION
OF THIS STATE AND NATION. PARTICIPATING AS
A VOLUNTEER IN AN EXPEDITION AGAINST INDIANS
AND TORIES, HE WAS KILLED FROM AMBUSH NEAR
THE KEOWEE RIVER, AUGUST 1, 1776.

BORN AN ARISTOCRAT, HE BECAME A DEMOCRAT,
AN ENGLISHMAN, HE CAST HIS LOT WITH AMERICA;
TRUE TO HIS ANCIENT FAITH, HE GAVE HIS LIFE
FOR NEW HOPES OF HUMAN LIBERTY AND UNDERSTANDING.

ERECTED AT THE TIME OF THE BICENTENNIAL CELEBRATION
OF THE JEWISH COMMUNITY OF CHARLESTON, 1950.

APPROVED BY THE HISTORICAL COMMISSION OF CHARLESTON, S.C.

Plaque commemorating Francis Salvador, behind the city hall in Charleston. Salvador died during the Revolutionary War and was hailed as a hero by George Washington. Salvador having been buried where he fell, this plaque stands in lieu of a grave marker.

In spite of the Jews' contributions to society, and even though Jews were allowed to participate in society much more freely in America than they had been in Europe, there was still much discrimination against them. Early American history has many recorded incidents of anti-Semitism. For example, in New York in 1743, a man so disrupted a Jewish burial that it made it impossible to bury the corpse. In 1746, the New York congregation advertised a reward for finding the vandals who had destroyed tombs and damaged the cemetery walls. Benjamin Nones, an American Jew, had to defend himself against an attack published in a Federalist paper, *Gazette of the United States.* In 1752, in Williamsburg, Virginia, an anti-Semitic stereotype was used to portray the character Shylock of Shakespeare's *The Merchant of Venice,* and was greeted with great applause. The performance was so popular it went on to play to audiences in Annapolis, Philadelphia, Charleston, and New York.

Not all of the discrimination came from outside the Jewish community. Some critical attacks came from within the ranks of the American Jews. In Philadelphia, Pennsylvania, a rift developed between two groups of Jews, and as a result Philadelphia was the first colonial city to experience two distinctly different congregations. The first to be established was Mikveh Israel, whose first shul was officially opened in 1783. This shul and its format were of the Spanish-Portuguese mode. In the late 1790's, a splinter group broke away from Mikveh Israel. Called Rodeph Sholom, it was comprised of Jews of German descent who felt discriminated against by the Sephardic community.

Freedom as we know it today was still a long way off, and the Jews of the colonies had to fight hard to win every freedom they received. Some, like Francis Salvador, gave their lives in battle. Many Jews supported and fought in the Revolutionary War, and later many Jews became abolitionists. Jacob Cohen, of Richmond, Virginia and Jacob Levy, Jr., of New York freed their own slaves early in 1773 and then went on to encourage others to do the same.

On August 17, 1790, Moses Seixas from Newport's Touro Synagogue in Rhode Island wrote to George Washington. His letter included the phrase, "a Government which to bigotry gives no sanction, to persecution no assistance." When George Washington answered Seixas' letter, he repeated that phrase as his own. Sent to New York, Savannah, and Charleston as well, this letter was the first official statement of the United States government denouncing bigotry.

The Jews clearly received a lot when they took the important step of emigrating from Europe to the American colonies. They were fleeing persecution and pursuing the opportunities of freedom, and they were largely rewarded.

But it is also important to remember that the Jews who settled in colonial America also contributed greatly to the new land, and later to the young nation. Their contributions in the fields of business, science, social reform, education, and the arts are clear to see. Equally important are their contributions to the political philosophy that has made the United States a land that

---

Following pages: Letter from President George Washington to the Hebrew congregation in Newport, Rhode Island. This is the first statement from the newly formed federal government concerning freedom for Jews in America.

To the Hebrew Congregation in Newport
Rhode Island.

Gentlemen.

While I receive, with much satisfaction,
your Address replete with expressions of affection
and esteem; I rejoice in the opportunity of assuring
you, that I shall always retain a grateful remem-
brance of the cordial welcome I experienced in
my visit to Newport, from all classes of citizens.
The reflection on the days of difficulty and
danger which are past is rendered the more sweet,
from a consciousness that they are succeeded by days
of uncommon prosperity and security. If we have
wisdom to make the best use of the advantages with
which we are now favored, we cannot fail, under the
just administration of a good Government, to become
a great and a happy people.
The Citizens of the United States of America
have a right to applaud themselves for having given
to mankind examples of an enlarged and liberal
policy: a policy worthy of imitation. All possess
alike liberty of conscience and immunities of
citizenship. It is now no more that toleration is
spoken of, as if it was by the indulgence of one
class of people, that another enjoyed the exercise
of their inherent natural rights. For happily
the

the Government of the United States, which gives to bigotry no sanction, to persecution no assistance requires only that they who live under its protection should demean themselves as good citizens, in giving it on all occasions their effectual support.

It would be inconsistent with the frankness of my character not to avow that I am pleased with your favorable opinion of my administration, and fervent wishes for my felicity. May the children of the Stock of Abraham, who dwell in this land, continue to merit and enjoy the good will of the other Inhabitants; while every one shall sit in safety under his own vine and figtree, and there shall be none to make him afraid. May the father of all mercies scatter light and not darkness in our paths, and make us all in our several vocations useful here, and in his own due time and way everlastingly happy.

G: Washington

espouses inclusion and liberty. Founded on belief in religious freedom, America represented a promise to the Jews. Eager to partake of this promise, the Jews of early America returned the favor by entering fully and participating in the growth of the new society.

What remains of the early American Jewish experience can be seen in the form of fine houses, portraits, silverware, preserved libraries, synagogues and cemeteries, and other examples of good taste. But if we take a second look, we find that the more important legacy is one of good deeds, and an earnest and energetic contribution to the political philosophy of tolerance that remains an essential ingredient of America's inheritance today.

Bibliography

I found the following books and periodicals to be a great source of information and inspiration.

Anon. *Publications of the American Jewish Historical Society: Lyons Collection, Voume 2, 1920.* Waltham, Massachusetts, American Jewish Historical Society, 1969.

Antiques Magazine, 1995–2001. New York.

Elzas, Barnett. *The Jews of South Carolina.* Charleston, South Carolina, Daggett Printing Company, 1903.

Herskowitz, Dr. Leo. *Letters of the Franks Family.*

Karp, Dr. Abraham. *The Jewish Experience in America.* Waltham, Massachusetts, American Jewish Historical Society, 1969.

Lebeson, Anita. *Pilgrim People.* New York, Minerva Press, 1975.

Levy, B.H. *Savannah's Old Jewish Community Cemeteries.* Mercer, Georgia, Mercer University Press, 1982.

London, Hannah. *Portraits of Jews.* Olympic Marketing Corporation, 1969.

Marcus, Jacob Rader. *American Jewry Documents—18th Century.*

————. *Early American Jews.* Philadelphia, Pennsylvania, Jewish Publication Society, 1951.

Pool, David De Sola. *An Old Faith in a New World.* New York, Columbia University Press, 1955.

————. *Portraits Etched in Stone.* New York, Columbia University Press, 1952.

Reznikoff and Engelman. *The Jews of Charleston.* Philadelphia, Pennsylvania, 1969.

Stern, Dr. Malcolm. *Jewish Genealogies.* Cincinnati, Ohio, American Jewish Historical Society, 1978.

Whiteman and Wolf. *Jews of Philadelphia.* Philadelphia, Pennsylvania, Jewish Publishing Society, 1957.

Index

Abrahams, Abraham, 77

Abraham, Chapman, 124

Adam, Robert, 128

Adams, John, 69, 132, 155

Adler, Cyrus, 116

Alcott, Louisa May, 108

Algonquin Indians, 28

American Jewish Historical Society, NY, 25,
86, 179

Amsterdam, 18ff, 27

Antigua, 97

Asher, Richa, 31

Ashkenazim, 21, 23, 34, 167

Baltimore, Maryland, 21, 25, 113–18, 173,
175, 178

   Stock Exchange, 116

   Museum of Art, 140

Bank of Boston, 53

Bank of North America, 103

Bank of Richmond, 126

Barsimson, Jacob, 25

Barton, Reverend Thomas, 83

Basurto, Diego Enriquez, 27

Beth Elohim, Charleston, SC, 171, 173ff,
182

Beth Shalome Synagogue, Richmond, VA,
45, 136f, 140–43, 145

Bevis Marks Portuguese Shul, London, 18

Bird, William, II, 69

B'Nai Jeshuruan Educational Institute, NY,
162

Boone, Daniel, 135

Boerhaave, Hermann, 66

Bols, Frederick, 35

Boston Athenaeum, 112

Boston, MA, 21, 45, 58, 107

Brick Presbyterian Church, NY, 40

British Parish Church, Williamsburg, VA, 65

Brown University, 57, 61, 182

Burwell, Carter, 68

Bush, Mathias, 77

Cardoso, Benjamin, 30

Carigal, Rabbi Hyam, 62

Carpenter, E.M., 112

Caribbean, 25, 60

Carvalho family, 173, 175, 178

   David Nunes, 173

   Sara Solis, 175, 178

   Solomon Nunes, 173–79

Charleston, SC, 21, 90, 135, 173ff, 182

   City Hall, 26

Charlottesville, VA, 21

Chatham Square Cemetery, 28, 31f, 39, 49,
121f

Clinton, George, 47

Cohen family, Baltimore, 113f, 116, 118,
132

   Benjamin I., 116

   Dr. Joshua, 116

   Israel I., 114

   Jacob, 25, 116

   Judith, 114

   Mendes, 116

   Philip, 116, 132

Cohen family, Richmond

   Esther Mordecai, 138

   Jacob I., 135, 138ff, 185

   Joshua, 138, 140

   Peschal, 138

Cohen

   Samuel Myers, 76, 83

   Elkalah, 77

   Richa, 76

Cohen, Mrs. Edward (Caroline), 143

Cole, Thomas, 178

College of Rhode Island, 182

College of William & Mary, 65, 132

   S.W.E.M. Library, 72

Colonial Cemetary, Newport, RI, 112

Colonial House Corporation, 134

Columbia University (Kings College), 119f

Connecticut, 44, 46

   Littlefield County, 44

Continental Congress, 84
de Costa, Isaac, 61, 107, 109
Croghan, George, 83
Custis, John Parke & Martha, 68
Daguerre, Louis Jacques Mandé, 176
Delancy, Oliver, 35
Delapleine, Joshua, 44
De Leon, Perry, 140
Detroit Institute of Arts, 61
Dropsie College, Philadelphia, 116
Du Pont, Henry, 79
Durand, Asher Brown, 178
Dutch Jewish Synagogue, Recife, 24
Dutch West India Company, 18, 20
Duyckinck, Gerardus, 24f, 35
England, 23, 25–28
Etting family, 113–18
    Benjamin, 79
    Elijah, 113
    J. Marx, 114
    Rachel Gatz, 113f
    Reuben, 114
    Salomon, 25, 113, 115f, 118
    Samuel, 116
    Shinah Solomon, 113f
Ezrath Orechim, 101, 141
Farmer's Bank of Virginia, 140
Fauquier, Governor, 69
Female Association for Relief of Women &
    Children in Reduced Circumstances,
    Philadelphia, 26, 79
Ferguson, Finlay F., Jr., 134
Ferdinand, King, of Spain, 17
First National Bank of Boston, 110
Fisher, Miers, 105
Fort McHenry, 116
Forty-first Presbyterian Church, NY, 41
Franklin, Benjamin, 75, 79
Franks family, 31–33, 35f, 75
    Abigail (Bilhah A. Levy), 31–36
    David, 35ff, 40, 47, 75f, 84
    Jacob, 32f, 35, 75
    Margaret Evans, 36f, 40
    Moses, 22, 101
    Naphtali (father), 32

Naphtali (son), 33, 35
    Phila, 35f
    Richa, 36f
Free Library, Philadelphia, 75, 79
Fremont, General John Charles, 176–79
Galt, John, 67f
Gaunse, Joachim, 20
George III, King, of England, 70, 97
Georgia, 21, 23, 90f, 95f
Georgia Historical Society, Savannah, 87
Georgia Union Society, 98
Germany, 23
Girard Bank, Pennsylvania, 125f
Girard, Stephen, 125
Gomez family, 27–30, 59, 61
    Antonio, 27
    Benjamin, 29
    Daniel, 29, 59
    David, 29
    Duarte, 27
    Isaac (father of Luis), 27
    Isaac (son of Luis), 29
    Jacob, 29
    Luis Moses, 27–30, 59
    Mordecai, 29
Gratz family, 75–81, 102, 132
    B & M Gratz Company, 76
    Barnard, 23, 75–79, 84, 113, 133
    Benjamin, 79
    Jacob, 81
    Michael, 23, 44, 47, 75–81, 84, 107, 133,
        148f
    Miriam, 26, 84, 148ff, 152
    Rachel, 79
    Rebecca, 26, 79, 81, 84
    Simon, 79
Gratz Liberal College for Arts & Sciences,
    Philadelphia, 79
Gratzville, KY, 79
Gratzville Park Community Center,
    Lexington, KY, 79
Grimes, David, 40
Halbrun, David, 105
Harby, Isaac, 183
Hart, Ezekiel, 120

Hart
  Amos, 159
  Isaac & Nephtali, 51
Harrison, Peter, 46, 52f
Hays family, 107f, 110ff
  Judah, 107, 112
  Judith, 110, 142
  Moses Michael, 45, 53, 55, 107–12, 142
  Rachel Myers, 107f, 111f
  Reyna, 107f
  Sally, 110, 142
Hays, Samuel, 103
Hebrew Benevolent Society of Los Angeles, 177f
Hebrew Congregation, Washington, D.C., 162
Hebrew Hospital, Baltimore, 116
Hebrew Library, 116
Hendricks, Harmon, 29, 149f
  Francis Isaacs, 149f, 152
  Uriah, 44, 149
Henry, Patrick, 69
Hepplewhite, Alice, 129
Holland, 18, 20, 23
Hudson River Valley, NY, 28
Huntington, Samuel, 99
Illinois, 83
Inquisition (Spain and Portugal), 17ff, 27, 57, 173
Institution for the Deaf and Dumb, Philadelphia, 121
Irving, Washington, 79
Isaacs, Isaiah, 135, 138f
Isaacs, Joshua, 45
Isaacs, Lazarus, 22
Isabella, Queen, of Spain, 17
Jacobs, Solomon, 140
Jarvis, John Wesley, 118, 157
Jefferson, Thomas, 68f, 136f, 139, 145f, 154f, 162f
Jewish Cemetary, Newport, RI, 62f
Johlson, J., 169
Johnson, William, 83
Judas Magnus Memorial Museum, Berkeley, CA, 165

Kennedy, Thomas, 116
Kentucky, 79, 81, 83, 138
Kingston, Jamaica, 53
Kneller, Sir Godfrey, 35
Kusinitz, Bernard, 55
de Lamerie, Paul, 35
Lancaster, PA, 21f, 77, 83f, 138
Latrobe, Benjamin Henry, 124, 129
Lauzada, Moses, 123
Lazarus, Emma, 30
Leicester, MA, 58, 61
Leeser, Isaac, 141, 167–72, 178
  Rehine, 168
Levy, Asser, 20, 25
Levy, Benjamin, 113
Levy, Moses Raphael, 23ff, 31f, 75
  family, 31, 175
  Bilhah Abigail (Abigail Franks), 31–36
  Nathan, 75f, 84
Levy, Uriah Phillips, 159–66
  Michael, 159
  Rachel Phillips, 159, 164
  Virginia Lopez, 161f
Levy, Virginia & Jacob, 185
Library of Congress, 162
Lincoln, President Abraham, 164, 178
Lincoln, General, 90
Lindo, Moses, 181f
Lloyd Street Synagogue, Baltimore, 178
Locke, John, 136
London, 18
Los Angeles, CA, 176
Lopez family, 58f, 61
  Aaron, 51f, 55, 57–63
  Anna (Abigail), 58, 61
  Catherine (Sarah), 58, 63
  Joshua, 53, 61
  Moses, 59
  Sally (Sarah), Rodriguez, 61
  Samuel, 51
Louden, Lord, 40
Lumbrezo, Jacob, 113
Lushington, Captain, 138
Madison, James, 105f, 133, 138, 154f, 160

Maimonides, 17, 179
Maimonides Rabbi Training College, Philadelphia, 170f
Malcolm, Alexander, 32
Marlboro, NY, 28
Marranos, 17, 27
Marshall, John, 144
Maryland, 25, 113, 116f
    General Assembly, 25
    University of, 116
Maryland Historical Society, Baltimore, 79, 118, 179
Marx family, 132
    Joseph, 132, 145
    Judith & Louise, 132
Masonry (Freemasonry), 45, 98, 110, 139f
    Grand Lodge of Massachusetts, 110
    King David Lodge, NYC, 45, 110
    Solomon Lodge, Savannah, 98
Massachusetts Mutual Fire Insurance Co., 110
Mears, Caty, 40
Mears, Grace, 31
Mears, Joyce, 40
Metropolitan Museum of Art, NY, 35, 41
Mickve Israel Synagogue, Savannah, 91, 95f, 99
Mikveh Israel Congregation, Philadelphia, 41f, 47, 75, 79, 86, 97, 101f, 105, 120, 138, 148, 159, 167–70, 185
Minis family, 87–93, 96
    Abigail, 87–91, 93
    Abraham, 87f, 91
    Esther, Hannah, Judith, Leah, & Sarah, 93
    Isaac, 91
    Judith Pollack, 92
    Philip, 87, 91
Monticello, 162ff
Monroe, James, 139, 160
Mordecai family, 141
    Ellen, Jacob, & Rachel, 141f
    Judith Myers, 141
    Moses & Solly, 142
Mordecai, Mordecai, 167
Moise, Penina, 182

Morris, Robert, 130ff
Moses
    Isaac, 40, 123
    Reyna, 40
Museum of the City of New York, 48
Museum of Fine Arts, Boston, 45
Myers, Moses & family, 123–34
    Abram, 125, 133
    Adeline, 125
    Augusta, 125, 132
    Elizah Judah, 124ff, 128, 130–33
    Frederick, 125
    Henry, 133
    Hyam, 123, 125
    John, 125, 131f
    Judith & Louise Marx, 132
    Mary Georgia, 125
    Moses, 45, 123–34
    Myer, 125, 132
    Rachel Lauzada, 123
    Samuel, 125, 132f
Myers, Samuel, 111, 123
Myers, Myer & family, 39f, 45ff, 142
    Asher, 40
    Elkalah Cohen, 40, 77
    Gustavus Aldophus, 144
    Judith, 39
    Judith Hays, 142ff
    Moses Mears, 111, 142f
    Myer, 39–49, 62, 77, 107, 110
    Sally Hays, 142
    Samuel, 125, 142–45
    Solomon, 39
Nathan, Grace Seixas & Simon, 147f, 150, 152
National Gallery of Art, Washington, D.C., 178f
Nassy, Dr. D., 183
New Amsterdam, 19ff
    Council, 25
New England, 21
New Orleans, LA, 54, 105
Newport, RI, 21, 25, 51, 53f, 57ff, 61f, 107, 135, 161

New York City (New York Colony), 20ff,
24f, 27–32, 34, 36, 39, 101, 107, 119–
21, 123, 132, 135, 155, 162, 164, 184
New York Gold & Silver Society, 47f
New York Historical Society, 40, 155
New York State, 21
New York Stock Exchange, 120
Noah, Mordecai Manuel, 153–57
Nones, Benjamin, 140, 184
Norfolk Academy, Norfolk, VA, 131
Norfolk Museum of Arts & Sciences, 134
Norfolk, VA, 21–124–28, 131–34, 166
     Common Council, 126
Office of Finance, Colonial Congress, 103
Oglethorpe, Governor James, 87, 95
Ohio, 83
Orphan's Society, Philadelphia, 79
Orphan's Society, Savannah, 95
Otis, Harrison Gray, 108
Pasteur, William, 67f
de Paz, Antonio Enriquez, 27
Peale, Charles Wilson, 114, 139
Peale, Rembrandt, 118
Pennsylvania, 21, 83, 121
Pennsylvania Academy of Fine Arts,
     Philadelphia, 79, 140
Perkins, Thomas H., 108
Petersburg, VA, 150f
Philadelphia Museum of Art, 114
Philadelphia, PA, 21, 23, 37, 47, 75–81, 84,
     86, 97, 101ff, 105, 120, 135, 140, 153,
     159, 167–71, 173, 185
Phillips, Jonas, 153f, 159
Phillips, Levy, 86
Phillips, Rebecca Macado, 148
Pittsburgh, PA, 84
Poland, 23, 83
Polk, Charles Peale, 114
Potter, Lieutenant William, 161
Portugal, 18f, 23, 27, 57
Portuguese Israelite Synagogue, Amsterdam,
     18f
Pride, James, 68
Public Hospital, Williamsburg, VA, 65, 69–
     73
Quaco, 63

Randolph, Edmond, 138
Randolph, George & Peyton, 69
Reade, John & Catherine Livingstone, 40
Recife, Pernambuco, Brazil, 18f, 24, 119
Redwood Library Literary Club, Newport,
     RI, 22, 53, 58
Reid, Mrs. Fergus, 134
Revere, Paul, 39, 45, 110f, 142, 144
Rhode Island, 60f
Ribeira, Dr. Samuel Nunes, 95
Richmond, VA, 21, 45, 113, 135–45, 168
Richmond Jewish Cemetery, 139
Ritson, Anne, 125
Rivera family, 57f
     Abraham, 63
     Hannah Pimental Sassportas, 58, 63
     Isaac Rodriguez, 63
     Jacob Rodriguez, 51f, 55, 57f, 59, 61, 63
Roanoke Colony, VA, 20
Rodeph Sholem Congregation, Philadelphia,
     185
Rothchild, Baron & Baroness, 162
Rush, Benjamin, 99
Salvador, Francis, 26, 184f
Salvador family, 26
Salomon family, 101ff, 105f
     Ezekial, 105
     Haym, 23, 101–06
     Haym M., 105
     Rachel Franks, 101
Samuels, Haym, 141, 151
     Rebecca Alexander, 141, 150ff
     Sammy, 151f
Sarzedos, Abraham, 107, 109
Savannah, Georgia, 21f, 87–93, 95–99, 135
School for the Deaf and Dumb, 81
Schuyler, Nicholas, 84
Scott, Sir Walter, 79
Seixas, Isaac B., Richmond, 140f
Seixas family, NY, 119–22
     Benjamin, 120
     David, 121
     Gershom Mendes, 119–22, 140, 147f,
          167
     Isaac, 40
Seixas, Moses, 185

Sephardim, 19, 21, 23, 34, 51, 119, 167, 171, 173, 178, 182, 185
de Sequeyra, Dr. John, 65–73
    Joseph, 66
Shearith Israel Congregation, 22, 28, 30–34, 39f, 40, 42, 45ff, 49, 55, 59, 75, 86, 107, 119f, 123, 140, 155, 161, 164
Sheftall family, 95–99
    Benjamin, 23, 96
    Francis Hart, 96
    Mordecai, 22f, 90f, 95–99
    Moses, 98f
    Nellie Bush, 98
    Sheftall, 97
Shield's Tavern, Williamsburg, VA, 72
Simon family, 77, 83f, 86, 114
    Bilhah Simon Cohen, 86
    Joseph, 77, 83–86
    Leah Simon Phillips, 86
    Miriam, 77, 84
    Rusa Bunn, 83
    Shinah, 84, 86
Smith, Nathan & Susan McIntosh, 41
Smith, Robert, 69
Solomon, Joseph, 113
    Shinah, 113
South Carolina, 21, 26, 87, 181f
    First Provincial Congress, 26
    Second Provincial Congress, 26
Spain, 17f, 23
    Cordova, 17
Spruce Hill Lead Mine, 44f
State Department, Washington, D.C., 45
    John Quincy Adams State Drawing Room, 111
Stiegel Glassworks, 22
Stiles, Reverend Ezra, 25f, 53, 62
de St. Mercy, Merceau, 126
St. Eustatius, Caribbean, 123
Stuart, Gilbert, 58, 61, 112, 128, 144
Stuyvesant, Peter, 20, 25
Sully, Thomas, 79, 113, 131, 164, 175
Thomas Jefferson Memorial Society, 163
Trinity Church, NY, 25, 28, 31, 53

Touro, Reverend Isaac, 53ff
    Abraham, 53, 55
    Judah, 53ff, 178
    Rebecca, 53
    Reyna, 53, 107
Touro Synagogue, Newport, RI, 22, 25f, 42, 46, 51f, 54f, 57f, 61f, 108, 185
United States Bank, 143
United States Navy, 160f, 164ff
Vermont, 44
Virginia, 21, 135–39, 141, 144, 146
    State Penitentiary, 139
    Historical Society, 144
Virginia House of Burgesses, 68
Warrenton, NC, 21
Washington, George, 23, 26, 68f, 84, 89, 91, 97, 104, 120, 140, 184–87
    Martha, 147
West Indies, 77
Williams, Roger, 51
Williamsburg, VA, 21, 65f, 68–73, 184
Winterthun Museum, Delaware, 80
Wright, General, 89f
Wylly, Colonol, 90
Wyner Museum, Temple Israel, Boston, 110
Wythe, George, 68f, 141
Yale Center of Art, 48
Yale Museum of Art, 48
Yale University, 25
Yeshuat Israel Synagogue, 51–54
York, PA, 21, 113f
Young, Brigham, 176, 178